T0110568

# Clothes Encounters of the Divine Kind

## Where Image Reflects the Truth

**DIANE DONATO**

**BALBOA.**
PRESS

A DIVISION OF HAY HOUSE

Copyright © 2014 Diane Donato.

All rights reserved. No part of this book may be used or reproduced by any means, graphic, electronic, or mechanical, including photocopying, recording, taping or by any information storage retrieval system without the written permission of the publisher except in the case of brief quotations embodied in critical articles and reviews.

Balboa Press books may be ordered through booksellers or by contacting:

Balboa Press
A Division of Hay House
1663 Liberty Drive
Bloomington, IN 47403
www.balboapress.com
1 (877) 407-4847

Because of the dynamic nature of the Internet, any web addresses or links contained in this book may have changed since publication and may no longer be valid. The views expressed in this work are solely those of the author and do not necessarily reflect the views of the publisher, and the publisher hereby disclaims any responsibility for them.

The techniques, ideas and suggestions in this book are not intended as a substitute for sound medical advice. They have been based on the personal experience and research of the author. The author makes no claim to be, and in no way is to be considered as practicing medicine in any form. Any application of the techniques, ideas and suggestions presented in this book are at the discretion, risk and responsibility of the reader. Any reference to healing in this work is to be interpreted as spiritual healing that often can impact other areas of healing.

Any people depicted in stock imagery provided by Thinkstock are models, and such images are being used for illustrative purposes only. Certain stock imagery © Thinkstock.

Printed in the United States of America.

ISBN: 978-1-4525-1885-5 (sc)
ISBN: 978-1-4525-1887-9 (hc)
ISBN: 978-1-4525-1886-2 (e)

Library of Congress Control Number: 2014912851

Balboa Press rev. date: 07/23/2014

# *Acknowledgments & Dedication*

Life with all of its many ups and downs brought me into contact with numerous human beings who served as my teachers in one way or another during my journey in this particular life form. You all have my whole-hearted thanks. Most of you will not realize that you have been my teacher. Some of you were what Carlos Castaneda would call 'petty tyrants' and for those who served me in that capacity I am eternally grateful. You kept me humble and made me stretch beyond my limitations. You may or may not know who you are and that's ok too. Others have supported me in all of my adventures and validated my entire being. I also thank you all very dearly.

Family has also played an amazing part in my journey – with both support and a lot of teasing – siblings have an amazing way of telling it like it is and I love the three of you for that. Especially big brother who always seems to rescue me, baby bro who always remembers to include me and middle bro who seems to create the balance I often need in my life with his wonderful calm manner. I also have four amazing sister-in-laws who have also always been there for me. Mom and Dad, who have already crossed over, were the best parents I could have ever chosen. They gave me the FREEDOM to explore and take risks in life and were always supportive with undying, unconditional LOVE. I know they are still guiding me from above.

And finally, my undying love and gratitude for my Teacher, Master Shaman – Keshav Howe, who, without the guidance, love and support, this work would never have happened. Thank you for giving me the tough love I needed when it was necessary without degrading me in any way, and for never faltering in your support for my awakening to my divinity. I love you.

Thank you God, Universe, and all the religions and beings from non-ordinary reality for what you have shown me along this pathless path of true awakening.

I love all of you from the bottomless bottom of my heart. This book is dedicated to all of you!

Thank you life!

With Love and Gratitude,
Diane Donato

# *Introduction*

It has been 15+ years after my first book "Attitude by Design" where I opened with the dilemma of whether or not to close my image consulting business, "Clothes Encounters". Well, I am here to tell you that while I have taken "breaks" from it, I never really locked the door on that venture and find myself now in the year 2011 reopening it with a brand new set of eyes as I begin this work. The door was closed for a while but left a wee bit ajar and never locked. It was left ajar just waiting for me to discover its true purpose, and yes, like the Phoenix, it has now been fully resurrected. In fact, it would appear that I am experiencing a resurrection myself. Why, resurrect it you might ask? I honestly do not know, however, perhaps because it is what I was born to do with my remaining time here on this earth.

I have found myself struggling to find my life's purpose for most of my life: in search of who I am, what I am supposed to be doing and with whom I am supposed to be doing it. In other words, is there a purpose to my life and will I ever truly know what that purpose is? One thing I do know for sure is that I love fashion, clothing and colors and I love playing with them. Always have and at age 62 (the beginning of this work) I still do.

I have always had a fascination with beauty, be it with make-up or clothing, jewelry and colors or even the decorations of a home or a garden. And yes, in nature as well, but nature was not my focus and serves more as an inspiration.

I have also struggled with the guilty feelings of how being concerned with outward beauty was being superficial and that what really counts is how someone is on the inside—inner beauty, kindness and compassion. I have often wondered why we simply couldn't have both!! And quite honestly, I truly believe that each one of us has the potential to appear externally beautiful with a little help from the cosmetic and fashion industries. I have finally come to the realization that actually looking beautiful on the outside helps us see our inner beauty when we look in the mirror; and being confident enough to express our inner beauty outwardly taking risks with our clothing by stepping out of our comfort zones can be the portal to our finding out who we truly are underneath our outward appearances and underneath our "thoughts". This is what I refer to as our divinity, which can also help us discover and decide just what is our life's purpose. Getting clarity on who you are ultimately can guide you to the discovery of what you are on the planet to do and learn. Interestingly enough, for me it has been discovering who I am NOT that has lead me to know who I am.

Speaking of our life's purpose: What if our purpose is simply to rediscover who we are and celebrate and communicate that throughout our lives? To rediscover our divinity! We all have spent a lifetime learning how to survive on the planet at the expense of losing sight of our true essence. It is my hope that this work will assist the you in your journey to discovering the truth of who you are and the best way to **express** that truth with the help of the use of clothing and colors to assist in attracting the people and situations that will lead you to know and fulfill your destiny (whatever you perceive it to be). The sole intent of this work is to assist you with your journey to FREEDOM and LOVE. Projecting the image that reflects your own truth opens doors to true freedom. I am not talking about the mind made "idea" of who you think you are, but actually who or what you are at your core essence.

This 13 feet train is a painting I did while in Kindergarten on my own (i.e. not an assignment) – I guess from a ripe early age I was fascinated with colors (the first 2 cars are black and the next 3 are red, blue and green consecutively) and trains. In the spirit of Cat Steven's music, I have named this my Peace Train.

Hindsight is always 20/20: Looking back on my life I have noticed that everything I have done has lead me to where I am today. You are more than likely wondering where that is. I like to look at it as a continuous journey to the realization of "Who am I?" The following is somewhat of my take on how each major event in my life that occurred or presented itself to me has led me to the essence of Diane. I call this '**unmasking the layers to the discovery of our divinity**'. This cannot be described in a word or words that anyone could understand, however by connecting the dots you should be able to see how finding out who or what I or we am/are or not peels away the layers of the onion of what we are not can lead to the discovery and realization of who or what I am/we are. Life is a journey not a result or a destination, it is a process of discovery. And my experience of it is that each moment presents itself with yet another opportunity to awaken to the discovery of who I am – the divine essence of Diane. Just what is the Divine Essence of Diane? Please follow the thread of my life and notice how clothing, colors and fashion have been a reflection of the evolutionary process of where I was at during different times in my life.

## Who Am I? Who are you?

Sharing my own journey down the rabbit hole to the discovery of the truth of who I am is the best way to begin. It is my hope that my journey will inspire you to venture out into the forest, down the rabbit hole, to the discovery of who you are and it doesn't matter what vehicle you ride during the journey. It's what is learned along the way that is important. My journey is best described with regard to my experiences with fashion and beauty... you might call it "Clothes Encounters" of the divine kind.

Just like any other story, background information is necessary in order for the true picture that is painted reveals itself. Life has a way of leading us to this discovery even when we are not consciously striving for it, at least that has been my experience. It is there right in front of us each step of the way if only we open ourselves to being able to see it. I defer you to the movie "What the Bleep Do We Know" and the scene about the ships arriving on the horizon and the inability of the Native Americans to see them – only the Shaman of the Tribe was able to see them, as a reference and further explanation of this phenomenon.

Please note that it is difficult to keep this work in the pure chronological order of my life because my own awakenings happened on different levels at different times. I have attempted to organize this work by decades and the reader needs to know that although I am talking in linear terms, my awakening happened in multiple levels of reality. In other words, revisiting it now has put an entirely new dimension and understanding of it that wasn't noticed back then.

# CHAPTER 1

# *The Beginning in Form*

I was born on April 15, 1949 at 2:53 in the afternoon, which happened to be "Good Friday" that year. I was raised as a Roman Catholic and I've experienced much wonder through the years at the fact that I had been born on the anniversary of Jesus Christ's death on the cross and at almost 3:00 in the afternoon, the time of His bodily death. My mother's best friend had written her a note upon my birth expressing how special I was to have been born on Good Friday. In my innocence, I took that to mean that I had a special mission on Earth, so on some level, my quest for finding truth began at a very early age. I felt responsible not in an egocentric way, but rather in a very humble way. I wanted to fulfill my destiny.

I loved Jesus with all of my heart and wept every Easter time during my younger years at His crucifixion (and became ill almost every Easter weekend). I celebrated His resurrection on Easter Sunday (and although I am no longer a practicing Catholic, I still do to this day. I often felt like I knew Him personally and on some level I did and still do (I think we all have some knowledge of Him regardless of how we were brought up). This belief stayed with me all of my life and continues even now as I am writing this. Because I was born on Good Friday, the day Jesus was crucified and died on the cross, I always feared that I would die when I was thirty-three years old (not that I ever thought I was Jesus or even like Him. I just loved Him and wanted to marry Him. I wanted to learn how to be just like Him). Yet, it is no accident that I met my first spiritual teacher on May 23, 1982 when I was thirty-three years old. This was the beginning of the <u>*death*</u> of the ego built image of Diane. But, I am getting ahead of myself. Unlike Jesus who *died* at age thirty-three, my spiritual journey *began* at age thirty-three. It is also important to note that my mother told me that she knew I was *different* from my older brother right away because I manifested from infancy a very free spirit. In fact, she had nicknamed me Bird, a name that stayed with me throughout my life. I remember her often referring to me as being flighty. I also remember her telling me that I was the one who had taught her that each one of us is different with different personalities, temperaments and gifts. Because she knew that I needed the freedom to develop my wings she did her best to provide that freedom to me as much as possible during that time.

When I was very young, I went on vacation at the beach with my parents. I remember my older brother was playing the accordion and getting a lot of attention. Suddenly I had the urge to get up and act like a conductor, leading him in his music. This action on my part garnered many laughs from the adults. I didn't want to play the music; I wanted to *lead* the band! I guess from at a young age I was destined to be a leader or conductor of some sort!

Fashion is my passion. My search for my true identity began in 1963, when I was in high school, and fashion played a huge part in this search. Actually, it was earlier than that. I recall that when I was in grammar school at Blessed Sacrament Grammar School I noticed the nuns' habits and the big rosary beads that hung from their waists. I particularly loved the wide cuffs at the wrist that allowed them to place their hands in them like a muff, and I thought the large rosary beads around their waist were very cool. I remember going home one day and telling my mother that I wanted to be a nun. She asked me why, and I responded that I liked their outfits. Mom told me that that was vanity and that was no reason to want to be a nun because they give up vanity when they take their vows. Another time when I saw a nun's wimple blow up in the wind and expose her bald head underneath, I was devastated. The desire to become a nun went away gradually after that. When I watched movies of the postulants scrubbing floors and waiting on the priests in the rectories, I realized that the life of a nun is not very glamorous. However, the clincher was when in the fourth grade I got slapped across the face by a nun teacher for erroneously putting my name on the wrong line on a piece of paper. My true direct experience of nuns was that nuns were mean and I didn't want to have to be mean. I still loved Jesus though and on some level I still wanted to marry Him. I also felt a strong connection to Mary Magdalene back then even though we were taught that she was a prostitute. I didn't believe that way back then, and now subscribe to what was revealed about her by Dan Brown in *The daVinci Code.*

Even though I was raised as a Catholic, I often questioned the teachings of the church. I remember being taught to *fear* God, and that if I walked into another church other than Catholic it was a mortal sin. I couldn't wrap my head around the hypocrisy of the Catholic Church. How could God be love and fear at the same time? Even though I attended an all girl Catholic college, I still didn't buy the Catholic religion. Yet, I am grateful for having learned about spirituality and God from a very young age. It served as a good foundation for my life's journey back to spirit.

Growing up, I had three brothers, a father and a mother. My mom wanted me to be able to do all of the things that she was not allowed to do growing up because she was female. Both my parents are of Italian heritage. My mom's parents came from Italy when they were teenagers. (I do not remember much about my father's family.) Mom was overprotected by her father, who was very old-fashioned. When Mom was younger and living at home it became fashionable for women to wear slacks. Mom was beautiful and loved beautiful clothes. One day, she bought a pair of pants and had them lying on her bed. When her father saw them he asked, who they belonged to. When she told him they were hers and that they were the latest style in women's clothes, he ripped them apart. Pants were only to be worn by men, he decreed. Because she was also deprived of her independence she wanted to make sure that I had mine. I was able to do and have all the things she was not allowed to do and have. She told me that she wasn't even allowed to roller skate with two skates, but rather only with one skate for safety. "Always keep one foot firmly planted on the ground" was his theory, I guess.

So for quite a while I was somewhat of a tomboy even though I always knew I was a girl. I liked being a girl. It seems that my earliest recollection of wanting to be pretty centered on my need to be loved. Everyone loved my mother and she was always referred to as being beautiful. In fact, she was a dead ringer for the then popular actress Hedy Lamarr. I thought that if I was pretty and beautiful, then people would love me because everyone loved my mother.

In my early teens I discovered a love for makeup and began wearing eye makeup in high school to make me look pretty. I realize now that this was the way I began emerging into my femininity. I realized I was a girl and wanted to be recognized as a girl and I wanted to be liked and loved as Mom was.

As I was writing this, a memory from when I was around six years old has surfaced. That winter we had moved into our first and only house that my parents bought. I was playing out in the backyard wearing the same sort of green hooded snorkel jacket like my brothers wore when two girls from the house behind ours were playing nearby and noticed me. One of them said to the other, "Don't go there! That's a boy!" I heard them and quickly yelled out after taking off the hood, "Hey, I'm not a boy. Look, I am a girl!"

They then came over to me, and we became good friends. I don't remember ever wearing that boys' snorkel jacket again!

There was a lot of testosterone in my house growing up, so I couldn't help catching some of it. It has served me as both a blessing and a curse throughout my life. I was always torn between being "one of the guys" and "one of the girls". I loved men. I loved being a girl. I also thought that if I was pretty enough then I would be loved by men and would find my soul mate/husband. Somewhere in there was also the need to be smart. Of course, I was right smack in the middle of the feminist movement. In 1971, I was graduated from college. I no longer wanted to be loved just because of my looks. Although I never thought I was pretty enough mostly because I wasn't petite. I was larger than many of the girls I went to school with. I figured I needed to develop my brain. I also have a brain. Interestingly enough I was raised in a wonderful Italian/American family. It bears repeating that Mom was absolutely knockdown gorgeous —and as mentioned earlier, a dead ringer for Hedy Lamarr, so everyone has told me from her generation who knew her. I wanted to be pretty like Mom. Dad was very handsome too. They made an elegant couple and were utterly devoted to each other. The earliest pictures of Mom showed her very highly fashionably dressed. She was way ahead of her time socially and intellectually as well. She was a very modern woman in spite of her overprotective Italian father and mother. My mother had told me that she knew my father was the man for her the very first time she met him (I believe they met at someone else's wedding), so in my own little way I always thought I would know instantly when I had met my soul mate. I made a lot of mistakes along the way with this belief. In my own little world, beauty translated into the ticket to finding true "love".

The following is a somewhat chronological account of my evolution by decades. As you approach the end of this work you will notice that the linear account of my growth and development no longer is relevant and you see how clothing and colors helped to integrate my body, mind and spirit into wholeness. I lump the 60's and 70's together mostly because they seem to merge together and explain the formative years of high school and college and the beginning of the "image" of Diane. Huge learning experiences about life, yet fashion hadn't quite made the huge impact on my life that it made a bit later.

# CHAPTER 2

# *The 60's and 70's High School and College & Boston*

During my high school years, fashion and clothing options were pretty much limited to either a "preppy" or "hoody" look. You were either a "clicker" or a "hood". The clickers wore their hair straight and wore tasseled Bass Weejuns (loafers) or saddle shoes and the hoods wore their hair teased up with high and tight fitting clothes and pointed shoes. Watch the movie *Grease* and you'll get the picture of the two different groups. I couldn't make up my mind so I was a little bit of both although my dress most of the time leaned towards the "preppy" or clickers. I had eclectic tastes even back then and I was always torn between wearing my hair straight or teased up and loafers or pointed shoes. I remember actually ironing my hair with my mother's clothing iron (flat irons had not been invented yet!!) and I remember using toilet paper rolls (before huge rollers were available) to set my hair on to assist in straightening it as well as teasing my hair so that it looked "big". So, I alternated as the mood or social function dictated. I had friends from both sides of the fence...I guess you could say I was neutral – like Switzerland. I accepted everyone for who they were rather than what they wore, and I wanted everyone to accept me for who I was. I dressed to fit in no matter what the occasion was. I had a keen sense of fairness and openness even back then that I have embraced for most of my life.

The Beatles became very popular when I was in high school and I loved them and their music. I had a few boyfriends in high school - and was really in love with an older boy named Ricky who I had met while driving around and hanging around on weekends. He was more of a "hood" and had a motorcycle which I loved riding on the back of. It should be noted that my parents had forbade me to ride on motorcycles, but I did it anyway, behind their backs of course. In school I was a "clicker" and out of school I was somewhat of a "hood", but not totally either one in either place. I couldn't pick sides and I wouldn't. I was open to all of life even back then.

When I turned 16 during my Sophmore year in high school I immediately got a job working in a Doctor's Office part time after school. I did typing of patient's records and occasionally assisted in the back room with the Doctor during examinations. I really enjoyed the job because it gave me some spending money however; it prevented me from hanging out at the "Handy Kitchen" restaurant where all the kids went after school. This was probably a blessing in disguise. I decided not to go into nursing even though I liked the job at the Doctor's Office. I wanted to go to a four-year college and perhaps become a high school math teacher like my Dad. During the 2+years I worked after school the Doctor and his Nurse often referred to me as "Sunshine" because I was always happy and up beat and loved working."

I must admit that I was your typical teenager and had issues with my mother and father at times. However, these were not the norm, and for the most part both parents supported me very well and I knew that I was loved by both of them. Yet, I did have a bit of rebellion in me.

One event that comes to mind was when the *wet look* raincoats were the rage and all the *in crowd* girls were buying them. I wanted one too and my mother told me to go downtown and charge one on her Worth's credit card. They were faux leather and the very latest trend. She told me not to buy the most expensive one or the cheapest one. I came home with one that was dark brown and a little bit shorter than I would normally wear. When my mother saw it, she hated it on me because it was way too short and didn't flatter me in any way so she took me downtown to take it back and find another one. I ended up with the most expensive one in the store in pure white and it looked fabulous on me. My mother wanted me to look my best and she proved it by getting me the very best (even though we didn't have a lot of money then).

I graduated high school in 1967 and went off to college that Fall. My weight had always been somewhat of an issue, but I was always told I had a very pretty face, however it wasn't until college that I actually went on my first diets and became more conscious of my body. College was an educational experience for me, more social/experiential than academic, although I did study a little and learned a lot. It was in college that my social consciousness arose with deciding to major in Social Sciences rather than my initial intention of becoming a math teacher like my Dad. This decision was helped along with the fact that a nun who was head of the math department met privately with students in her room and I was too cool to be meeting with a professor after school. Fashion did not play such a major role in my life then, although I did enjoy new clothes when my family could afford them and I always wanted to look pretty. The fashion and glamour world was relatively simple then: a few cosmetics and a couple of nice outfits to wear to a dance, to church and on holidays; not to mention that it was ok then to wear the same things over and over again. It was great to have 5 different outfits to wear to school each week. My mom and I wore the same size for a while when I was in high school and college and she had a really sharp orange burlap skirt suit that I loved and wore on occasions. I was always allowed to buy back-to-school outfits in the fall and on Easter outfit in the spring along with a few new spring and summer items.

I also remember my parents allowing me to go to Boston with a friend for a weekend during the summer of 1967 to shop for a few new outfits for my first year in College. It was so much fun, shopping on my own in Boston. I remember buying two outfits for College with shoes to match. One was an orange and greenish-beige striped knit dress with very cool orange shoes to match, and the other was a two piece striped navy blue and white skirt set with navy blue shoes to match. These were my basic "back to school outfits" for College and they were very stylish. These were the outfits that I wore to the Friday and Saturday night socials at our brother College. Although as a teenager in the 60's and 70's there weren't so many fashion choices, there were definitely images that we bought into. I remember wearing Bass Weejuns and Saddle Shoes too as I mentioned before and I also remember madras plaid being very popular. Madras plaid was a cotton material that actually bled when it was washed and I remember this being a good thing. It was cool that the fabric bled. My guess now is that it more than likely is named after the then English city of Madras in India, now known as Chennai and more than likely was manufactured there.

My college was St. Joseph's College in Standish, Maine, an all female Catholic College. Most of my high school friends who attended college went to school in Boston, so I spent many weekends visiting them in Boston. Because of my free spirit, my mother wrote me a blanket permission slip that said I could spend any and all weekends off campus without further parental permission. Back then dressing was very casual, with an occasional dress and heels for attending the social dances that were hosted by our brother schools up in Maine. My two new outfits were simply perfect and I loved wearing them. It was a different time. We didn't have the extensive wardrobes that we have today and we wore the same outfits frequently. I was conscious of looking my best, but was not obsessed with it then. We always wanted to look neat and clean and pretty and were not as concerned with wearing something new and different every day like we are today.

It should be noted that I attended a college that was also attended by one of my good girlfriends from high school and grammar school. She was very glamorous and dressed beautifully. She was petite and simply very pretty. I had always wanted to look like her and attract the boys like she did, but I simply never thought I was pretty enough so I stayed more in the background supporting her in her many adventures. I was tall and always had a large frame. This pattern of staying in the background was one I followed in high school as well with my very best friend who always had great boyfriends, and I am still very close with her to this day. It is interesting, as you will see how my path evolved over time, although still with the common thread of fashion and beauty operating behind the scenes.

In August of 1969, during summer break, at age 20, my best friend and I went to the Woodstock Music and Arts Festival and it was around that time that I truly identified myself as a "hippie" and began questioning the "establishment". We had a blast and my memories of it are vague with only a few highlights: I remember them saying over the PA system "if you took the green acid come immediately to the med tent", because it was bad acid and the kids were getting sick on it. I saw only one naked man, and I remember parking our vehicle on the median of the highway and walking many miles to get to the festival gates that had already been knocked down. We rode on hoods of cars at times to get there and I distinctly remember the towns people out on their lawns giving us food and water from their garden hoses. There was absolutely no violence. It was so very peaceful and loving- a REAL HAPPENING!! Everyone participated including the police. To this day I still have my ticket to Woodstock, which bears the price tag of $7.00.

WOODSTOCK MUSIC and ART FAIR
SUNDAY
AUGUST 17, 1969
10:00 A. M.
$7.00     Good For One Admission Only
P 00189
NO REFUNDS     GLOBE TICKET COMPANY

Not long after Woodstock I was at college in Maine when the military infiltrated Kent State College and murdered four college students (I believe Crosby, Stills, Nash and Young did a song about it where it mentions "tin soldiers and Nixon's coming, we're finally on our own, this summer I hear the drumming-four dead in Ohio." We were devastated!! I believe it occurred on May 4, 1970, and I do remember being at College on campus when the news arrived. This was terrifying to all college students across the country...

As mentioned earlier, while in College I initially had wanted to major in math and become a math teacher like my Dad, but when in college I learned about majoring in Social Sciences and loved the idea that a Social Worker helps people who want to help themselves. It sounded more noble than simply teaching math, hence I connected with spirit and a social consciousness with my career goals. I guess you might say that I had somewhat of a noble attitude that "I" could help those less fortunate than me.

Note: I was what you would label a Hippie yet, I was torn because my older brother was drafted into the Army and ended up serving a year in Vietnam. I was protesting the war at home while at the same time worrying about and praying for my big brother. It was a very strange place to be emotionally and I often felt very guilty about both the protests and loving my brother.

Even then I couldn't choose sides totally! Fortunately he came through without any injuries and leads a very successful life as an attorney now.

*Note: I also served as Vice President of the Student Government Association during my senior year and along with that post came the responsibility of being the Chairperson of the Social Probation Board. Although I didn't know it at the time, this prepared me for one of my most difficult careers in state government as an Equal Employment Opportunity Director with responsibility of investigating and rendering decisions on discrimination complaints. I guess Leadership of some sort has always been in the cards for me. Today it manifests in my Holistic Image Consulting business.*

During my senior year at college I met and fell in love with a guy from Maine Maritime Academy. We dated for quite a while and things were hot and heavy, however, I had wanted to be a virgin when I got married and would not go all the way with him. He became very frustrated and broke up with me because of that. I was so hurt and angry that a few months after he broke up with me I went out, got drunk and had sex with I guy I didn't even know until that night. It was my first one-night stand. A very stupid way to lose my virginity! It didn't do anything for my self-respect, and I am sure hurt me throughout time with my other relationships with men. This really destroyed any self-esteem I previously had about being worthy of love because of all the guilt associated with not being a virgin anymore and not being married. It is interesting and sad how our conditioning about good and bad can destroy our self-love. Guilt is a very destructive emotion, and yet it is used to motivate us to 'right' action. I guess this is an example of the saying that 'your weakness can be your strength and your strength can be your weakness'.

Upon graduation from college in the summer of 1971 I moved to Boston to "find myself" as I told my mother and father who were upset that I would be leaving home and living on my own in a big strange city without being married. I wanted freedom and to be on my own even back then. Mom had always told me that she recognized that I was a free spirit from when I was an infant. Life was very different back then. And I grew up fast!! Still fashion played an important role yet it was not my primary focus. I am not sure what my primary focus was then except to work, have a good time and "find myself" and not necessarily in that order. I worked in an insurance agency that insured college tuitions, doing office and clerical work until they realized that I might be good at going on the road in sales.

I remember having bought a fantastic patchwork plaid dress with a little bit of lace trim by the designer Betsy Johnson when I lived in Boston...Oh how I loved that dress and wore it quite frequently. I often think back about it and wish I still had it. I would love wearing it today. I have been having retro experiences back to the 60's much like some of the youth of today. It was the time of the birth of the peace movement and not long after the development and communication of the peace sign. Boston was a time of experimentation for me...experimentation with sex and only minimal drugs. I was one of the fortunate ones who were afraid to try anything other than marijuana, hash and diet pills as speed occasionally. While living in Boston I met a man who went by the name of "Spider" and dated him a bit. He was different from any other man I had met and I really liked him. I started seeing knick-knacks with spiders on them and actually bought a set of glasses with spiders and web designs on them. Then I bought my very first car – a Karman Ghia that was hand painted red and black with a black widow spider painted on the roof. That car never died. It was fun to drive. I am one of the very lucky ones who did not get addicted to any drugs for which I am eternally grateful. I see how seductive they are and would not recommend anyone try them at all. They are just NO GOOD. I was very daring back in those days and one time while living in Boston, I also almost got myself raped while leaving a nightclub with a young man I had met that night. He didn't realize that no meant no, until I got hysterical and then he stopped and took me home and advised me to stop teasing because men do not really believe that no means no and that some day I will get raped if I am not careful.

Another event in Boston that knocked some sense into me (this time literally) was when I was out on a Friday night with friends, and had a very bad cold. Some guys I didn't know real well said they would give me a ride home but wanted to stop at another bar for a nightcap, so I went along with them in order to get the ride home. They ran into a so-called "friend" of theirs and we sat in a booth and started telling jokes. My joke (which ironically I can't remember now) topped this stranger's joke and he got mad at me and swore at me and I called him a male chauvinist F#@#; then he slapped me across the face. I got up from the table and walked away towards the bar and another stranger at the bar who had seen the whole thing from across the room said to me "how can you let him do that to you?" and then I picked up a glass and threw only the liquid out of the glass across the room and got the guy who had hit me right in the face with the liquid. He then picked up an "on the rocks" glass and hurled it across the room and hit me on the forehead splitting my forehead open, knocking me out. While I was unconscious I remember hearing a voice in the back of my head saying "GET UP DIANE, GET UP!" It wasn't anyone at the bar saying it, it had come from somewhere inside of me I guess. I often wonder if I had actually died and came back to life? Not sure. When I came to, the guy who threw the glass had run away and someone took me to the hospital. Seven (7) stitches later, a concussion and two black eyes I was on my way to a full recovery. This happened on December 7, 1972. The guy that did it had an alias and it was hard to find him, but the cops did find him several days later and I had to identify him and press charges. I ended up dropping the charges when he agreed to pay my medical expenses after using F. Lee Bailey's Law Firm to settle. I elected to not have the plastic surgery to hide the scar because the plastic surgeon said they could only make it a little thinner and I figured, just let it be, so I did. I received a whopping $195 as a settlement to cover medical expenses. That event didn't dampen my spirit or scare me enough to move back home.

My time living in Boston was from the summer of 1971 through December 1973 when I moved back to Connecticut because of a lump in my left breast that the doctor in Boston wanted to remove surgically. As I may have mentioned before, during my last two or so years in high school I had a part time job after school working for a well known surgeon in Waterbury, CT, so I decided that if I was going to have surgery on my breast he was going to do it, so that's what prompted me to move back to Connecticut. Upon seeing my doctor in Connecticut he looked at the mammogram and decided to take me off the birth control pill and wait 3 months and check again. In 3 months time it was gone so no surgery was necessary. I escaped unnecessary surgery simply by listening to the voice within me to go back home and see the Doctor whom I trusted wholeheartedly. It's funny how that inner voice speaks to us. We should be tuned in to listen to it more often.

In January 1974 one of my friends and I drove down to Key West, Florida and camped out there. I had bought a 4 or 6 - person tent and took $200 with me (a lot of money back then). While in Key West I met a man named "Mark" (can't remember his last name now) and fell "in love". I remember sleeping in the tent on coral in Key West and going to Sloppy Joe's Bar just about every night and drinking Southern Comfort whiskey shots that were lit up in a flame. I also remember seeing a man walking his pet Iguana on a leash and taking the Iguana swimming with him in the water. It should be noted that in the 70's while living in Boston I often wore a long cotton print skirt with a denim blue loose fitting poet's blouse and a head wrap/scarf tied around my head much like a gypsy. In fact, I had a portrait done of me in a scarf tied around my head which I still have hanging in my office. I also almost always wore a shawl. I was like a gypsy woman. And I still wear shawls and head gear often even today. I loved Cher's song about "gypsies tramps and thieves". The following is a portrait done of me in Provincetown, Massachusetts during the summer of 1972 in my head wrap. I loved that scarf and wore it often until I melted it while ironing it – Dang!!!

I also almost got married to Mark on a whim, but something that I cannot explain made me say goodbye to him and return to Connecticut with my friend. Once back in Connecticut in the winter of 1974 I got a full time job in an insurance agency that was owned by a bank. Another friend of mine and I got an apartment together in Waterbury. It was around this time that I went on one of my many diets and lost a lot of weight. Along with that weight loss came a new confidence in dressing. This began my dressing in "high fashion" and I began shopping in a new boutique that opened up in the Mall in Waterbury. The shop was known as "Ups and Downs". I bought very cool pantsuits by "Roncelli" and it was around that time that Disco Dancing became more popular and I wanted to learn that as well. I remember buying a sexy red halter-top dress with 1920's fringe around the bottom. I felt wonderful in my new body and began meeting and attracting more men. I even left my job with the insurance agency to try my hand at Retail so I applied for and got a job at Ups and Downs as a Store Manager. My District Manager was ruthless and I did not get along with her at all, so I ended up quitting that job and then getting a job at Bradlees' Department Stores as a Department Manager and did very well at it. I was having a ball wearing high fashion clothes with my new body and the love affair with fashion began in all its glory. I partied hearty in my new body image and clothing confidence and on August 1, 1975 while serving as a volunteer Black Jack Dealer at a fund raising event for hemophilia in the form of a Las Vegas Night on the ferry boat from Bridgeport to Port Jefferson, NY I met my soon to be husband. It was a fairy tale type of a meeting. I had been on the cruise and brought along a date with me, however, my date was off mingling while I dealt black jack at the tables. I had a couple of drinks of scotch on the rocks while dealing blackjack when the boat did a 360-degree turn. It was very hot and I was about to pass out when I saw this man that I had noticed was with some of the sponsors so I signaled for him to get me a relief. I subsequently passed out with my arms and head over the chips to prevent anyone from stealing them. In a funny romantic way he rescued me. I was a damsel in distress. However, that was the last I saw of him that night because my date came back and I was off with him for the rest of the night. The very next day I got a phone call from my rescuer who had gotten my number from the sponsors. He asked me out on a date and we went out to dinner and had a fabulous time.

We dated for quite a while and he seemed to be having difficulty getting a job in Connecticut so he took a job in Colorado and I threw him a going away party. I missed him terribly and one night after going out with one of my girlfriends I came home and called him on the phone crying that I missed him. We talked for a while, hung up and I went to sleep. Several hours later I woke up to someone sitting on my bed, shaking me, saying "Wake Up Diane, Wake Up Diane". It was him. He drove all night from Colorado without stopping to make sure I was ok. Now that is what I call "LOVE". It was amazing. He did move back from Colorado and we saw each other almost every day after that until we got married on October 8, 1977, two years after we had met. My parents threw me a beautiful wedding-the wedding of my dreams. My gown was modeled after my mom's wedding dress in an elegant simple soft knit flowing material and I wore a white gypsy looking scarf around my head instead of a veil.

From 1975 through most of 1977 I had been working full time as a Department Manager for Bradlees Department Stores in the fashions for women soft lines. However, around the beginning of 1977 was when the blue laws began to be changed in Connecticut and all retail stores were opening on Sundays. As mentioned earlier, I am from an Italian American family, and as is commonly known "family" is very important in Italian families and Sunday afternoon dinners were a weekly family event. I did not want to miss them. Simultaneously, the laws regarding collecting Unemployment Insurance were about to change so that if you "quit" a job you would be unable to collect unemployment. I had decided that I wanted to try to get a job more in line with my degree in Social Sciences, so just before my wedding on October 8, 1977 I quit my job in retail, got married, went on a honey moon driving throughout New England, came home to Waterbury, CT and proceeded to look for a job.

I was fortunate, and found a job as the Personnel Officer/EEO Director for the Waterbury CETA Administration and started in January 1978. I was very successful in the job and received commendations from the U.S. Civil Service Commission who had trained me in merit principles of personnel administration, the U.S. Labor Department and the EEOC. I stayed on the job for approximately a year and a half when my husband was able to land a business opportunity with income right away up in Vermont, so in July 1979 I quit this job and moved to Vermont to be with my husband. We lived in Quechee, Vermont in an apartment next door to a small cemetery while my husband was part owner of an Inn in Vermont. Vermont is very rural and Waterbury was a small city of 105,000 and had many more job opportunities than Vermont did. The only job I could find in Vermont was in sales as an employment recruiter based only on commissions. I took the job and disliked it immensely. I was bored in Vermont and began going to the one and only nightclub in the area that had dancing and began dancing the "hustle" with one of the son's of the owners of the Inn in Vermont. We got pretty good at it and actually introduced it to that area. I had some very pretty dance outfits that went with the hustle: Fringe looks like from the roaring 20's. Things were also beginning to deteriorate with my marriage and I wanted to move back home to Connecticut. I moved back to Connecticut and subsequently we dissolved the marriage.

Although I cannot put a date on it, I also remember having a fascination with the origin of my name, Diane, and found out that it was a form of the French translation of the name of the Roman goddess Diana and I read up about her. The name Diane means *divine*. Artemis was the Greek goddess version of Diana. I am also unsure of just when my fascination with the gods and goddesses of ancient times began, but I do remember being very young and being allowed to stay up late with my Dad to watch the various movies of the ancient times which centered around Greek and Roman mythology and Bible stories, and I always said that even though my ethnic background is Italian, I wanted to go to Greece, before going to Italy. I actually went to Greece in 1984, 27 years before going to Italy. I earned the trip with my sales and recruiting while working as an Independent Cosmetic Consultant for Aloe Charm, Inc. I also remember while in College I dressed up for one Halloween as a goddess in a white one-shoulder toga (I used a white bed sheet-photo enclosed) to express the goddess aspect of my essence. I used to imagine myself as one of the goddesses portrayed in the various movies. Venus De Milo comes to mind rather vividly.

I wanted to be beautiful because as you will recall I had thought that I would be loved if I were beautiful. Unfortunately, I always had somewhat of a weight problem, but it didn't consume me until I moved back to Connecticut from Boston in January of 1974. Yet it should be noted that my confidence with boys centered on my not being over weight, and along with that my confidence in dressing. It was when I lost weight (some time during 1974 and 1975) that I began to become fascinated with clothing and colors (as mentioned earlier) and seemed to attract men, and began to experiment with them (men and clothes-LOL).

I was able to keep the weight off throughout my marriage and I began to have confidence that was based on my outward appearance rather than on an inner knowing or true feeling of self worth. Hindsight again tells me that this was a false sense of confidence. During our dating time my husband had taken a job out in Colorado and I got to go and visit him there. I brought my newest high fashion clothes with me only to be avoided like the plague by the people out there. It was an amazing experience. My fiancée told me that the culture out there was very laid back, casual, outdoorsy, and country. It was cowboy territory and I was dressed like New York City to them and very intimidating. This was to be my first lesson on how you dress has a huge impact on how people respond to you and that the "culture" of the location also has an impact on how one is perceived in their dressing.

My idol in music and fashion during the 70's was Cher. In fact, my husband looked somewhat like Sonny Bono and I looked a bit like Cher, so our friends occasionally referred to us as Sonny and Cher. I remember wearing a very sexy black wet look low cut jumpsuit that was something Cher would have worn. Disco dancing was beginning to become popular some time around then too. I loved dancing and was fascinated by Disco Dancing as was made popular in the movie starring John Travolta, "Saturday

Night Fever." My recollection of fashion and glamour at that time was that it was beginning to make a larger presence in society, but it wasn't until the 1980's that I remember an extreme societal emphasis on our physical bodies (other than cosmetics because cosmetics have been 'in Vogue' since the beginning of recorded history). This coincided with the emergence of Olivia Newton John's song, "Let's get physical" and the openings of various health clubs across the country. In fact, I too got on the band wagon and joined a fitness center in 1988 at the age of 39... However, keep in mind that mankind throughout history has been decorating the body to delineate rank and status...tribal cultures as well as other cultures so we should not minimize the impact of clothing and colors on the evolution of humanity. We have been conditioned from early existence to use clothing and colors as communication tools.

One can see that it will soon become readily apparent that my true in depth spiritual journey began almost simultaneously with my delving into the area of fashion and beauty with my career that began in October 1980. Star Wars and Saturday and Night Fever were two of my most favorite movies during the 70's. You can also see that I had my feet in both the world of spirit and the world of form/fashion in the 70's. I loved the look of the dresses and the dancing in Saturday Night Fever and went to Disco Night Clubs and learned how to do the hustle pretty well, if I do say so myself.

The movie Star Wars came out in 1977 and introduced me to "the force" and with that I also managed to maintain somewhat of a contact with spirit. I absolutely loved the movie and actually still own the trilogy on VHS.

## Chapter 3

# *The 1980's*

Early in the spring of 1980 while still living in Vermont, I learned that my previous job with the Waterbury CETA Administration was open again due to the person who replaced me not liking the job. My former boss phoned me in Vermont and offered the job back to me knowing that I was unhappy in Vermont. I accepted the job and moved back to Connecticut in March 1980. My husband and I divorced in 1981.

It then seemed that almost all the men I became involved with drank alcohol to excess and it bothered me, so a friend of mine suggested that I go to Al Anon. It was in Al Anon that I learned I had no control over anyone else's drinking and I surrendered to my higher power in Al Anon. I learned the serenity prayer and employed it religiously. "God grant me the serenity to accept the things I cannot change, Courage to change the things I can, and the Wisdom to know the difference." Anonymous. I am eternally grateful for all that I learned around those Al Anon circles. Once I surrendered and reconnected to spirit and attended meetings for quite a while, I began to heal and relinquish my need to control, period. I am eternally grateful for having heeded this call from spirit and thus began the process for me to begin to look within myself rather than outside of myself to make changes. I did the 12 Steps of Al Anon with a vengeance and new founded freedom began to emerge.

Having had to deal with the illness of Alcoholism in others oddly enough was a portal to renewing my spirituality. It was the silver lining in the clouds of my being involved in dysfunctional relationships. Without sounding redundant, hindsight has told me that it truly was another wake up call from spirit. It struck like a bolt of lightening! I was still looking to find myself.

It is often said that the events that we perceive as negative things happen in our lives often are the portals to the discovery of the truth, i.e., the gateway to spirit and the discovery of just who we truly are in our essence. All paths seem to lead one to the path one needs to follow on their journey back to spirit. All we need to do is to open ourselves up to the pointers that the universe provides. This means opening up to everything that appears in the present moment and without judgment. I am eternally grateful that I had the presence of mind to pursue my path and although there were times when I stumbled off the path, I am eternally grateful for the nudges along the way that spirit has given me to help me get back on the path. It is a pathless path, one that one has to be open to noticing and everyone's path is unique to them. It truly is NOT the same old imitation game. My experience also has shown me that it can't truly be planned out, because as John Lennon once said "Life happens while you are making other plans!"

I also remember that looking good always made me feel good, whether it be with wearing make-up daily or just wearing a new outfit. This goes back to my childhood memories of getting a new outfit for Christmas and Easter. These were "special" days that required a "special outfit". (Perhaps this was the beginning of my feelings about why not make EVERY DAY SPECIAL WHICH HAS LEAD TO MY DRESSING CONSCIOUSLY EVERY DAY.) As I matured into a teenager I also remember that I never felt complete if I didn't have my make-up on that day. It was a must, a very important part of my morning ritual. At that time in my life, makeup was more important than the clothes. I like to compare it to our Native Americans putting on face paint before going to war, or before going out to hunt for food.

My next big career opportunity in the area of fashion and beauty began during October of 1980 (at that time we were still married and he had taken a job in Texas upon moving back from a brief time of living in Vermont). In October 1980 I found myself at a home demonstration show featuring "Aloe Charm Cosmetics" and found out that the company was looking for consultants to sell and represent their products. They also provided free training in the art of make up and running a business as an independent cosmetic consultant with them. Because I was alone yet still married, I had time on my hands, and I was intrigued about the business opportunity to become a Cosmetic Consultant. I had always fantasized about what it would be like if I owned my own business. I was fascinated with learning about the "healing" properties of Aloe Vera Plant and its miracle Gel. It was learning that the Aloe Plant was known as the "medicine" plant, the "healing" plant, and the first aid plant that really hooked my attention.

In the past I had difficulty in using other skin care lines and the consultant from Aloe Charm advised me that that was probably because most other lines had fragrance in them, and the Aloe Charm skin care line was fragrance free. I tried it and absolutely loved it. I was hooked on the product and hooked on the business opportunity. This was my very first connection to learning about healing with nature and outside of the realm of seeing a physician. It was the beginning of my awakening to nature and spirit. I loved wearing make-up and had time on my hands in the evenings (I was still married and did not want to go out to bars at night while married) so this part time opportunity was just perfect for me. My first book, "Attitude By Design" outlines some of my journey with Aloe Charm and how it brought me to having a positive attitude, my love of public speaking and healing, as well as continuing my spiritual studies. This career in sales with Aloe Charm introduced me to many motivational speakers and self help books, which I feel were very instrumental later on in my finding my way into the New Age sections of the bookstores. One of the first authors I became familiar with was Dr. Norman Vincent Peale with his "Power of Positive Thinking" and his other books. The authors and their works and tape series were a bridge to spirit for me. I won't repeat the story from my other book, but rather this program will show my journey down the rabbit hole to the discovery of my true essence pretty much from that point on and how fashion and beauty helped me to discover the truth of who I am and gave me the courage to express that truth both verbally in my communications and non verbally with my clothing and colors.

Aloe Charm trained us to never cancel a show because the hostess will not reschedule if we cancel it. We had a motto like in the theatre: "The Show Must Go On". My experience in life also is that 95% of success is simply "showing up". I remember one evening driving to a show during a snowstorm when fear gripped me on Interstate 84 and beginning to ask Jesus for help. In a split second, a total sense of peace enveloped me as I felt him sitting in the passenger seat of my car. I recognized this as a beautiful acknowledgment from spirit. I was fine from that point on and the show was a success too. Working with Aloe Charm made my fashion passion blossom. I began buying and wearing gorgeous hats. At first I wore them to give me confidence and later as I became more successful I wore them because I actually had more confidence. I have often referred to my hats as my "confidence hats". Although this journey down the rabbit hole is a sole/soul journey (pun intended) there has been much support from the universe along the way. It wasn't all as glamorous as one might think, and the challenges along the way simply pointed me back to spirit at every opportunity. At times I didn't always recognize the pointer, so spirit continued to give me more pointers. Yes, we do need to take our life's journey towards enlightenment alone, however, support is everywhere along the path and we will recognize that support once we open ourselves up to seeing it.

During 1983 I earned enough sales and recruiting requirements to not only be promoted to Manager but also to go on an all expense paid 10 day trip to Greece in 1984! I always knew that I wanted to travel to Greece before going to Italy, even though my ethnic heritage is Italian. My fascination with the Greek gods and goddesses was very profound from a very young age. While in Greece I had some mystical experiences while walking up to the Acropolis. I had an incredible experience of Déjà vu and an amazing experience of feeling like and having been a goddess. ***Thinking back now I am realizing that it was my first direct experience of my own Divinity- a truly divine experience.***

Being a child of the 60's and 70's I was considered to be a "hippie" or "flower child" as I mentioned earlier, and attended peace rallies and moratoriums during the late 60's and early 70's. There was a certain "image" that was portrayed in the clothing worn at that time which basically identified one as fitting into that label. Essentially, headgear or headbands and peasant shirts and skirts, flowers—free-flowing clothing that expressed a free flowing spirit of peace and love was the attire that communicated that essence. Free love was pretty much born then, perhaps out of the Vietnam War, along with the mantra of "make love, not war", "flower power" and of course there was the experimental use of drugs to bring us to higher states of consciousness. I won't explore drugs in this book, because drugs really didn't play a large part in my path to enlightenment, although I did experiment with marijuana and hash on occasion. You can read various works by Ram Dass or watch his movie *Fierce Grace* to learn more about the use of drugs during that time to clear up any misconceptions about the why and wherefore of their use during that era.

After my divorce I indulged in indoor roller-skating, fully embracing the cool clothing and accessories of that sport. Tight fitting jeans and colorful leg warmers were the "look" for skating at that time. This was my diversion from the loss of love at that time and a way to meet with and connect with others. Looking back I can see how this was a way to avoid looking within myself for the love that was missing in my life.

Then on May 23, 1982 at the age of 33 I met a man that I fell in love with. The meeting occurred while I was in Boston on a business trip for my full time job. I had gone up a day earlier to spend a night visiting one of my childhood girlfriends who was living in Boston. We went to a fundraiser dance for a charitable group and the theme of this was a "preppy dance". It could not be further from the truth that I would be considered a "preppy" at that time especially in my style of dressing, but we went to the fundraiser anyway. While at the dance I noticed across the room a tall man encircled in a white mist and had an immediate feeling of the presence of Jesus. It was a profoundly mystical experience that surprised the hell out of me (literally I think) yep (Another call from spirit). This was an amazing overwhelming and profound feeling of the presence of Jesus. Note: in fact, there was no so called "mist" around him from ordinary reality. I had been gifted with seeing his Aura without even knowing at the time that it was his Aura! A few moments later, on his own, he came over to me and we started talking and I think we danced a bit. We went out for coffee with my friend after the dance and exchanged phone numbers. I learned that he was a healer and spiritual teacher and follower of Rudolph Steiner, the founder of Anthroposophy. We dated a bit (he lived in NYC at the time and I in Waterbury, CT- it became a long distance friendship). However, I was in love with him and he became a spiritual "teacher" of sorts as I began studying the works of Rudolph Steiner and Anthroposophy that he had introduced to me. I had a lot of difficulty understanding Steiner and the limited contact with my friend who served somewhat as a teacher, was not enough to keep me grounded. I felt guilty about exploring spirituality outside of the Catholic Church because I remember being taught that it was a mortal sin for Catholics to go into any other than Catholic religious churches or read books that were not authorized by the Church, etc. After winning/earning a long deserved trip to Acapulco, Mexico in May 1985 and taking him along with the extra ticket I had won through my sales with Aloe Charm Cosmetics, at the end of the trip he told me that we were just friends!! I was devastated, but stoic about it, not allowing myself to cry or feel the despair. I put on my conditioned "big girl" tough act. However, the rejection I felt was staggering. I continued my studies with him via phone and I even joined a study group (at his suggestion) that met weekly in NYC on Wednesday evenings and I drove into NYC (75 miles away) alone each week at night after work - A very brave undertaking. I so wanted to "get" spirituality and on some level I was looking for his approval as well. I think he had moved to Atlanta, Georgia around this time. The study group was studying various Eastern religions and that was the first time I had ever actually heard of Hinduism. At that time in my life I was very left brain oriented and took everything I studied quite literally. I wasn't even getting the Hindu trinity of Brahma, Vishnu, and Shiva – by taking the interpretation of the trinity too literally. Two months after returning from Acapulco on the 4th of July 1985 (interesting that it is Independence Day and my ex husband's birthday) I crashed and had what I call a "nervous breakdown" which centered on extreme fear and massive feelings of guilt for studying spirituality outside of my having been raised as a

Catholic. At least that was what I thought at that time. Keep in mind that I hardly ever went to Sunday Mass and didn't follow Catholic rules any more, however it was odd that I would feel guilty about my studies outside of Catholicism. I believe the catalyst for this was the rejection of what I had hoped would be a long lasting love relationship with my spiritual teacher. Actually, I felt guilty about everything I had ever done, thought I was evil and was going to hell. I went so far as to ask my mother to call for a priest because I thought I needed to be exorcised. The drama was intense, to say the least. Yet, when the priest actually came, I was so frightened I wouldn't even open my mouth to talk. I thought I was being brainwashed, when in actuality, Catholicism had already brainwashed me! While I did know my name, address and phone number I really did not know who I truly was. I was completely and totally lost!! What I remembered and learned much later (2004+ or so) with the help of my current teacher (Keshav Howe-you will learn about him later) was that at the time I had been praying to know God, and to transcend my EGO and this was actually happening – EGO was dying and it was terrified and the FEAR I felt was the falling away of the EGO which I stopped in the process by seeking professional help. I realize now that I had to go through this process back then in order for me to fully continue on my journey. A huge broken heart actually turned out to be a portal to my learning about spirit and connecting with it. I did not have a teacher with me to help me through the process at that time. At that time I had no idea that I was on the discovery of Diane's inner spirit. I highly recommend that when you decide to embark on the path to your divinity you connect with a Teacher who can help you along the way. My role in this work and in my Image Consulting business is simply as a bridge to help you decide if you want to pursue inner peace and harmony. I have absolutely no regrets about anything that has happened along the way. My mother was very smart, and on that day (July 4, 1985) she asked me if I wanted to go and get help at the hospital, and I said "yes". As we were leaving for the hospital, I made myself fall down the stairs, thinking that I had to go to the emergency room in an ambulance physically incapacitated. I was all mixed up! My brain was swimming. I played dead a bit, but remember winking at my father that I was really all right. They called the ambulance and took me to the hospital. I was sedated and remember waking up in a locked room in the hospital, with sheets cut off from around my wrists (I guess they tied me down in the ambulance). I remember my mother being there when I came to after obviously having been sedated and looking at my wrists that still had remnants of the sheets that were tied around them to keep me from falling out of the bed in the ambulance and saying to her "look Mom, they made bracelets out of the sheets, they must have known how much I love jewelry". My sense of humor was still in tact. In fact, even though they kept me heavily sedated in the hospital, I managed to recognize how the experience I was having in the hospital was exactly like that explained in Ken Kesey's book, *One Flew Over the Cuckoo's Nest*. I knew I had flown over and wanted to get out – to the point where I recall even trying to get out of the window! (Of course this was an impossible task). I was hospitalized and made a quick recovery with the help of medication. When I knew I would be in the hospital for more than a day or two I had my parents bring me some clothes and make up because I could not stand the thought of wearing a hospital gown or the same clothes every day, not to mention going without makeup! I had three knit outfits comprising skirts and tops that were basically the same style in different colors that I loved wearing. These were the outfits I had Mom bring to me in the hospital. One was white, one was blue, and one was yellow. Even while in the hospital I wanted to dress up and look nice.

Also, I shave my legs and my underarms every day and I insisted on being able to do this. Sharp objects are not allowed in psych wards! However, they compromised with me by allowing me to shave with a razor as long as a nurse could supervise me doing it. I also remember that the mirrors in the bathroom were not made of glass and they were dark and it was difficult to see yourself in them to put on make up. I knew I had to get out soon! My total stay in the hospital was 19 days, with being released on weekends and the ability to go back to work on a part time basis from the hospital. Upon discharge they required that I see a psychiatrist as a follow up therapy. I did live at my parent's house for a few weeks after being released from the hospital. This too was a comical situation. My mother had broken her foot by tripping over a coffee table and couldn't walk very well, and I couldn't think very well, so I walked for her and she thought for me. I likened it to me being like C-3-P-O (the robot from Star Wars) because the heavy medication I was taking made my joints stiffened. I did recover and was back to work full time in a few weeks. The diagnosis at that point was that I had an "acute psychotic episode". I learned later that my recovery would only be temporary and would be a very long process. However, I did manage to stay out of the hospital for 8 years before another episode hit. I did give up all of my studies of Rudolph Steiner for quite a while because I had thought that it was the studying outside of the Catholic Church that caused the breakdown (Remember, I felt so guilty about studying spirituality outside of the church that I went so far as to call in a priest because I thought I needed to be exorcised!!!) and when he showed up at my parent's house I wouldn't and couldn't say a word to him, he suggested my parents take me to the hospital-which they did). I lived in constant fear that the breakdown would reoccur! In reality I now know that it was truly the loss of my spiritual identity with nowhere to turn for help that was the problem. I remember telling my older brother, the attorney, about my studies with this guy and gave him my teacher's phone number. My brother called him and very nicely asked him to never contact me again. He obliged and I never tried to contact him and told myself I wouldn't try to contact him for at least 10 years.

However, the desire and pull for a real connection to spirit was still pushing me to explore spirit so after a while I did contact him after 10 years and we have communicated on and off since then via phone and email, although I have never seen him since the return flight from Acapulco in 1985). During the time he and I were friends he had left NYC and moved to Atlanta, Georgia and we had communicated somewhat via phone. He is now married and lives in Texas.

**(Note: my Director in Aloe Charm cosmetics told me that she noticed that the more depressed I became the more make up I would wear – can you see how much how I used cosmetics and clothing to help me heal on the inside?)**

I still could not give up the quest for spirit though, so I looked for a more gentle approach, one that could be understood by a novice in spirituality. I found several authors such as Shakti Gawain with a more gentle approach to spirituality that I knew I needed. I cannot remember when I started with her work – 80's or 90's? They were spiritual books with less emphasis on good vs. evil; and books that were easier to understand than those that related to Steiner. I never lost my love and connection to Jesus Christ, but knew deep down there was more to spirituality than what the Catholic Church taught. I knew this deep in my soul a long time before picking up a book outside of the Church.

Through my studies I learned about the Eastern religions and studies around the 7 Chakras, or energy centers of the body and the color associated with each one of them. I also had a fascination with the Indian culture and loved the clothing that the women wore: The light, wing like, bright, flowing skirts and veils. I wanted to wear them! Are you getting the picture of how clothing and colors reflect the essence of a culture? The Indian culture is mired in spirituality and their clothing is bright, light, and flowing, while the American culture is rooted in materialism and our clothing is structured, firm and form fitting – the image of "control" comes to mind.

Simultaneously with my career in cosmetics was the music of Madonna that I loved. In fact, I had become somewhat of a "material girl" when it came to clothing and jewelry. I couldn't get enough of it. It became a substitute for the lack of the love of a man in my life. I loved Madonna's brassiness, courage and boldness. I thought that it was pretty bold of her to take on the name of "Madonna" in light of the Catholic Church's doctrine.

After my 1985 psychotic episode, some time in 1987 I decided to actually create my own accessory business and founded "Clothes Encounters". This creation was a form of "therapy" for me after the "nervous breakdown". I was a wee bit bored with the cosmetic business. I also remember waking up early one morning around 3:30 A.M. with the inspiration for the philosophy of Clothes Encounters:

"World peace is a worthy and viable goal which I know each of us has in the back or front of our mind. And it all starts with each one of us... You do make a difference!

When we feel good about ourselves, we in turn treat others better. When others are treated better, they in turn treat others better. It's a chain reaction. Looking good generates compliments, compliments raise self-esteem;

self-esteem creates confidence;
confidence increases healthy communication;
healthy communication creates harmony;

harmony brings World Peace."

Note: I believe it was around this time that I truly became a shopaholic with an obsession for clothing and jewelry, however some of this was truly legitimate buying for selling in the business. Yep, it definitely was a substitute for the lack of love I was experiencing in my life without a man, yet this one was a very healthy outlet. Bear in mind that throughout my time with Aloe Charm and Clothes Encounters I was also working a full time job in a city social service agency.

Buying jewelry only seasonally for Clothes Encounters was somewhat of a problem for repeat customers who had seen my inventory and had already bought what they wanted at the first or second shows they attended. Additionally, at my shows I concentrated on showing the jewelry, belts and scarves and taught a few scarf techniques. I had difficulty explaining the 'what' and 'how to' of what I was doing because I am an artist in that way and dressed and coordinated my outfits totally intuitively. I had not been able to codify it into a process. Fortunately a customer told me about the Karla Jordan Kollections jewelry company and that I might like to hook up with them because they taught the art of accessorizing, not to mention that I would be able to buy jewelry on a regular basis at their resource centers right here in Connecticut. This would assure fresh new inventory regularly. I found a representative and signed up to be a representative and through my affiliation with them met a woman who turned out to be one of my very best friends. It was with Karla Jordan Kollections that I began learning about the healing properties of the various stones. This further enhanced my desire to work with healing with nature. Her Kollections were made of natural and semi precious stones and the jewelry was all artist designed and made in limited editions. I began to learn about the healing properties of natural stones. The training I received in accessorizing is priceless. It was all the things that I had done with my own accessories intuitively, however, it was presented in a neatly organized technique that anyone could learn in a few moments. I found myself getting "stoned" on learning about stones and nature.

In 1989 I took a leap of faith and left my full time, so called "real job", and tried to live on my business alone with a small supplement of income from substitute teaching. This leap of faith was the result of my intuitive insight into matters of inappropriateness that I sensed yet again, intuitively, at the agency where I had been working. I knew it was time to leave. It is funny how the universe often points us in the direction we need to take without our doing too much thinking about what to do next. Unfortunately, my savings and home demonstrations only sustained me for about a year and a half before I went into some $13,000 credit card debt and needed to take action. I also had done some substitute teaching during this time as well for some extra income, but it simply wasn't enough to keep me out of debt. I had to now pay for health insurance, mortgage, car payment, and maintenance of the house as well as business expenses.

My intuitive insight into the inappropriateness of the agency turned out to be correct because a year or two after I left, the Federal Government came in and shut down the agency. There was a huge investigation into the agency mostly about misuse of funds and many people lost their jobs and a few even went to jail. My intuition turned out to be right--true spiritual guidance!!

Sometime after 1985 I had also started going to local singles dances in the hopes of meeting a new man. During that time I met a guy who I thought I fell in love with and I made it a point to hang out with him and his friends. I tried to go wherever he would go. We dated a bit, however, it never went anywhere. He was around 6 years younger than I was at the time and apparently looking for a younger woman to be more serious with. We used to all hang out at a night club in Waterbury on Friday nights and this one particular Friday night I wore an outfit that wasn't exactly figure flattering on me and he told me I had gotten fat and looked awful. It actually was the outfit that made me look like I had gained weight. (At this time in my life my weight was within the normal range for my height and build- I was not overweight) I was devastated so when I left happy hour to go to the other nightclub that evening I changed my clothes into a more flattering and sexy outfit. It was some time after my divorce that I became totally obsessed with how I looked. This coincided with my involvement in the cosmetics and fashion industry. However, I think a big part of it had to do with wanting to attract a new man in my life, and hindsight is telling me I went about in completely the wrong way. I had become obsessed with beauty, looking beautiful and having a sexy body. What happened as a result of this obsession on my part, which was very superficial, was that I attracted men that were interested only in sex. These men were without any real substance. Yet, inside of me, in spite of this obsession with beauty was a little girl who just simply wanted to love and be loved. Deep down there was a feeling of "unworthiness" that I couldn't identify concretely at the time. I thought if I was beautiful, then men would love me. I was unaware of it at the time, and it wasn't until years later that I was able to identify what was at the root of my suffering. I was so tied into my looks at that time it was pathetic. Don't get me wrong, I still take care of how I look, however, I no longer let my looks "define me". I was in the thralls of needing approval everywhere at that time. I never felt good enough and was always striving for perfection in my appearance thinking that looking good would bring me the happiness with a mate that I had been looking for. I was desperate!! I became a shopaholic, buying jewelry and clothing to nurture myself as a replacement for the love that was missing in my life and trying to make me loveable and worthy of love. The "nervous breakdowns" had also crumbled any self-confidence I had developed in my life until I was able to redefine them as "nervous BREAKTHROUGHS".

During the time I was substitute teaching I met a woman who wore hats and was very fashionable. She was a home economics teacher and had won an award for being national teacher of the year due to her creating a consignment shop in the school to benefit children with cancer. She was awesome and she introduced me to St. Theresa and I was once again reminded of the call from spirit. She said that if we prayed to St. Theresa to send a rose, and we name the color, when she would hear our prayers a rose of that color would show up in some form or another within a day or two. And you know what, it always did. One time, just to test it because I thought it was way too much of a coincidence, I prayed for a black rose. The very next day I received a flyer in the mail on pink paper with a Black Rose as the artwork on the top. I received the answer to my prayer for the black rose. I do not think this was a coincidence. In fact, today I do not experience anything as a coincidence, only that whatever happens is part of a divine plan that unfolds only in the moment. However, it is important that we be unencumbered enough to be open to notice the holy moments. They (the confirmations from spirit) are here all the time just waiting for us to notice.

Due to a dual career for most of the 80's I did not have much time to get to the movies, however, I did rent some of the more popular ones: The Princess Bride and the Indiana Jones movies beginning with Raiders of the Lost Ark. These contributed to connecting to spirit as well. I am now quite the movie buff and I truly recommend that everyone be sure to go to the movies regularly. They are wonderful pointers to the connection with the divine spirit in everyone and everything. Movies like Star

Wars, the Indiana Jones movies, Avatar, Alice in Wonderland, I AM, The Way, Inception, etc., all of them have deep messages to communicate when we simply open to what they are expressing. One needs to look below the surface of what is happening on the screen to the 'essence' of what is at the core of it. Life is much more than what meets the eye. Seeing with the eye and seeing with the "I AM" can be two very different experiences. Fashion also needs to be explored and seen from both the outer and inner perspectives.

# CHAPTER 4

# *The 1990's*

Some time in 1992 the politics in the City changed and the agency that had been shut down was reopened and all jobs were posted as new vacancies. I knew I needed to improve my finances and so I applied for several of the jobs that were announced and I was offered one of them. I accepted it and refinanced my home to pay off that credit card debt. So, while working full time again, the time to devote to my business had once again decreased. This was a rescue I like to attribute to the universe responding to my needs at that time. (Note: As I look back on my life I now see how the universe has always been there for me with support in one form or another just when I needed it.) I couldn't count on the income from my business to sustain me, so in 1995 I almost folded it, and thus began the writing of my first book "Attitude By Design" which I self published and is still available directly through me.

During the 90's I began to have the courage to begin pursuing my spiritual studies yet once again. As my confidence began to build again, I courageously went into the New Age sections of the book stores and had learned of a book called "A Course in Miracles" and bought it and attempted to read it and do the work in the book. The book as I recall was a channeled work that helped one to shed their EGOs. I did not understand this at all because I had always thought that I needed to build up my EGO. I was confused once again. The second breakdown happened while on a vacation in Nashville, Tennessee while upping my meds via Doctor's orders. I went to Nashville around

1993 while deeply immersed in Country Western Dancing and, of course, wearing the clothing and colors that coincided with that culture. Upon return from Nashville I went into the hospital. This hospitalization was a horrible experience at a hospital where I believe I was mistreated. I won't go into detail here, but let it suffice that I had been hospitalized on two other occasions since then and refused to go back to that hospital. The other experiences were most helpful.

My recollection is that this breakdown began with buying "A Course in Miracles" and attempting to read it and understand it without the help of a teacher. I once again became fearful of spiritual studies because I had misinterpreted much of the writing. I was in need of a teacher, but didn't realize it at the time. I thought that reading books would help me "get spirituality". Spirit calling me has always been playing in the background for me. A Course in Miracles also was very confusing and allegorical and I had difficulty comprehending it, but stubborn that I am (and glad that I am) I kept going into the New Age sections of the bookstores and stumbled upon the works of Shakti Gawain as mentioned earlier, beginning with her work on positive affirmations and such. I cannot remember all of her books, and I am unsure of the dates all of this reading and exploration took place, but I did buy all of them and read them and have continued reading spiritual books by various authors to this day. I was now experiencing much joy and connection to God and spirit so I kept up with my reading. I still had difficulty in traveling and fell apart a few times during the 90's, the first while on a vacation in 1993 in Nashville, Tennessee. It had been 8 years since my first "nervous breakdown". It seems that there were 3 things connected to my "breakdowns": 1, going on a vacation, 2. weight loss by going on a diet (to look good on vacation), and 3. Having had sex with a new man and him not pursuing the relationship. When all 3 things happened simultaneously, Diane fell apart. It was like the perfect storm. Guilt and low self-esteem were extremely prevalent during and for a long time after these episodes. I now view this part of my life as my version of the Rolling Stones' song about the 19th nervous breakdowns; only for me with each break down came a rewarding break through, not always obvious at the time, but breakthroughs none the less. In the 90's my spiritual studies increased tremendously because I was still experiencing a "lack" in my life. Outwardly I thought it was because I did not have a steady boyfriend or husband. True Love was missing. I had the love of my parents and my brothers and their wives and children, but somehow something was still missing. For sure I didn't love myself, and now more than ever because I felt flawed having now been labeled as having bipolar disorder by the psychiatrist I had been seeing since 1985. It seems that my psychiatrist couldn't or wouldn't connect my episodes with events in my life. He said it was "chemical" and that I was born with it and will die with it. On some deep level, I **knew** this was not exactly true. I knew the breakdowns were connected to events in my life that were giving me a teaching that I just didn't get at the time. Yet, in spite of this, I was able to continue working successfully in both my business and my full time job. **More importantly I still dressed impeccably.** I continued to buy clothing and jewelry as a substitute for the love that was missing. It is an addiction that I am able to keep in check today. Today, the urge to go shopping serves as a pointer to me that I am avoiding something or resisting something and/or feeling a lack in some area of my life. It is an invitation for me to meet whatever I need to meet to become present. It seems that shopping had become the avoidance of my being in the present moment. It is me running away from me and has been my method of avoiding getting to know the true essence of Diane. This is something we all do in avoiding our true divinity and each of us does it in a different way. (Perhaps more on this later) There is a paradox here because fashion has also played a HUGE part in my healing. Funny how your weakness can be your strength and your strength can be your weakness!

With the speaking experience I gained through my affiliation with Aloe Charm and Karla Jordan Kollections came a burning desire to help empower others to achieve their life's goals and to do it via public speaking. I created a workshop on the Empowerment of Goals and was able to present the workshop through my work in the employment and training programs we operated at the Workforce Connection through the Labor Department for Dislocated Workers. It was a great success. Then in February of 1996 my mother died at the age of 72 after a one-year battle with lung cancer. I was devastated at the loss of my mother. I remember while lying in bed the night she passed away, seeing briefly and feeling her spirit actually come into my bedroom. It seemed she wanted to be sure I was ok. For me this was a sign that only our bodies die, our spirit lives on in other realms. Although I was devastated at losing my mother when she was so young (72), I was comforted at having been raised by a loving family who instilled in me the belief that the world does go on regardless of what happens. I increased my spiritual studies and learned about the Omega Institute of Holistic Studies in Rhinebeck, New York from my best friend growing up. I obtained a catalog for the 1996 offerings and found a class on "The Art of Empowerment" taught by David Gershon and Gail Straub at the Omega Institute in Rhinebeck, New York in the summer of 1996. It was a week long training on how to conduct empowerment workshops while at the same time learning how to empower yourself to create the life that you love. This workshop was absolutely perfect for me at the time. I was able to revise the Empowerment of Goals Workshop (I had created and held at the Labor Department's Career Center as part of my full time job) to include some of the concepts and techniques I learned at the workshop at Omega and my workshops were even more successful. I began to learn how to access spirit by way of guided imagery.

I find it interesting that once you connect with "intent" and "commitment", the Universe responds appropriately with opportunities that are congruent with that intent. This began my love affair with Omega and my commitment to healing myself and re-igniting my connection with spirit and finding myself. This first workshop at Omega helped me to realize my dream of conducting empowerment workshops for others who had lost their way while at the same time helping me to heal myself. It is often said that the teacher teaches what she needs to learn and I am living proof of this concept. I was also able to use what I learned in this workshop in my clothing business as well. Little did I know that this journey that I thought was to help others was actually going to lead me to helping myself through one of the first steps on my path of the discovery of who I am. After the first night of the workshop at Omega, while lying in bed, I could hear a song playing off in the distance. On the second day of the workshop the trainers played that same song during a journey. I was awestruck to the point that I asked them if it was playing around the campus the night before. They said not to their knowledge, and that I probably had had a premonition about the song. I learned it was "Ode to Joy" and I adore that song to this day. Today I am realizing that "Ode to Joy" is a song I need to embrace and play more often.

*Diane Donato*

> At one point in the 2010 movie "Alice in Wonderland" the Mad Hatter told Alice "It's all about YOU, you know". Little did I know that life is all about me, not in a egotistical relative way, but rather in an absolute sense with regard to questioning the whys and wherefores of events and life helping to lead me to discovery of who I am. It's never about the "others", they are simply mirrors pointing back to you, or me as in my case. I love the concept that when you point your index finger at someone there are 3 other fingers pointing back at you. It's all about you/me. More about me and Alice and the journey down the rabbit hole later.

During my affiliation with Karla Jordan Kollections (a jewelry and accessories multi level marketing company-no longer in business) I met and trained with image consultants from all over the country. I took extensive trainings in *Color Analysis, Rainbow Personality™, Semiotics,* and accessorizing. I also studied with Jan Larkay, author of the book *Flatter Your Figure.* I studied extensively color diversity and color power with an image consultant from California and simultaneously my spiritual studies at that time introduced me to Eastern philosophies and the 7 Chakras, or energy centers of the body that included the color that is associated with each of those energy centers. This was my first true conceptual link of fashion/clothing and colors to spirit. I was fascinated by the connection. Initially Clothes Encounters only involved the selling of jewelry and accessories through conducting in-home presentations on the art of accessorizing. Once I began my studies in color and image with the other Image Consultants that I came in contact with through Karla Jordan Kollections I expanded my business to include workshops on the meanings and messages of clothing and colors, and dressing to flatter your figure. I also learned about the healing properties of the various natural stones, which often is linked to the healing properties of the colors that they are. This has now evolved into my true interest into using the healing properties of clothing and colors and being able to express one's true essence with the freedom to express oneself. It's interesting how I tried on all of the "images" regarding the "roles" I played in life – roles regarding jobs as well as social activities. I was motivated to be the best at everything because I believed that being the best would bring me approval and ultimately love. This is how living in a society that conditions one to be competitive manifested in me. I emerged myself whole-heartedly in everything I tried on. I wanted them to "fit" and I wanted to be the very best at whatever I did because I thought when all this happened, then I would be loved. However, my best was never good enough for me as my inner critic. I was like one of the ugly stepsisters in the story of Cinderella trying to "fit" in the glass slipper as it related to my choice of careers and other interests. I was always searching – not always sure of just what or who I was in search of.

Some time around 1992 or 1993 I became interested in Country Dancing through one of my friends who simply loved it. So, I spent just about 6 evenings a week dancing at a country western night club called "Illusions" in Wolcott, Connecticut - only a few miles from my home. I guess you could say I took a big hiatus from my business at that time for a few years as I dove head first (or rather feet first) into the dancing with a vengeance. I loved it. I embraced the whole image of it. Of course, I bought fabulous country western clothing and approximately 8 pairs of cowboy boots, as well as a few cowboy hats to go with the outfits. I may have been the best-dressed country dancer in the state! I actually became very good at the 2 step and other partner dances as well as line dancing and lost a lot of weight doing it. In fact, this was the only period of my life when I could eat anything I wanted to and didn't gain any weight. In the late 80's and early 90's I wore many suits to work and while in my country dancing mode I wore them with cowboy boots. I had very high-fashion colorful and stylish cowboy boots to go with whatever outfit I was wearing to the dances. My friends from dancing gave me the nickname of "rhinestone cowgirl" because I always worked in cool blingy jewelry and accessories with my country western dance outfits. I actually had a denim jacket filled with silver studs on the collar and down the front lapels and on the cuffs. My passion for fashion stayed with me regardless of what phase of my life I was in. It was and continues to be one of the constants and passions in my life. I realize now that in actuality I truly love fashion. I also became very fond of country music and one of my favorite country songs is *The Dance* by Garth Brooks. Another favorite of mine that stays with me often is the one that goes like this by John Michael Montgomery: "Life's a dance, you learn as you go, sometimes you lead, sometimes you follow. Don't worry about what you don't know, life's a dance, you learn as you go." Both songs hold very deep profound truths in the lyrics. As time went on my interest in country dancing began to fade along simultaneously with the break up of a band that we used to follow. Yes, I was also a groupie of sorts. The band was called "Wild Horse" and they were phenomenal! It seemed all of the friends I had made stopped going to the dances when the band split up and it phased out with our group. I also lost a friend that went to Nashville with me during that time because we had to return early due to the breakdown that happened when I travelled with her in Nashville. She was a trooper in getting me back to Connecticut (we had driven down in her car) and in dealing with my psychosis at the time. I am eternally grateful to her for her strength and still feel sad that our friendship had to end up falling apart because of my dis-ease. Yet, we all move on and things happen the way they are supposed to happen. I have no regrets!

Always in the back of my mind was the belief that if I dressed really nice and looked really pretty all of the time people would love me. In fact, I also held the belief that in order for me to meet a man I had to be beautiful and look like a movie star or a model. I strove for this with a vengeance never believing that I was beautiful or movie star quality yet still trying. Many people have told me through the years that I should have been a model, however, I never thought I was pretty enough, thin enough or good enough to be a model. My mother even thought I would make a good model especially on QVC. I also had the belief that I had to have a beautiful body in order to feel worthy of the love of a man. I keep repeating it here because it was and sometimes is a deep seated belief that I needed to shed. And at times it revisits me giving me the opportunity to heal it on another deeper level. I was looking for love in all the wrong places and couldn't find it anywhere. In fact, now I truly see how my hunting for love simply pushed it farther away. Upon leaving the country-dance scene I started writing my first book "Attitude by Design" in 1994 and self published it some time during 1996. I did a few local book signings and sold some at various bazaars and to friends and affiliates from various networking groups I was involved in. After I self-published "Attitude by Design" I found that I could not abandon my business totally, so I simply stopped doing it for a while and continued to pursue my spiritual studies. Funny how "Attitude by Design" was intended to be a bridge for readers to cross over into spiritual studies, and how it truly served as a bridge for me to cross over to going deeper into my own spiritual studies.

My mother's passing away in 1996 brought about my beginning to face my own mortality. I also was aware that I had no money set aside other than what Social Security would pay me when I retired and no pension from my job for retirement, so I began taking examinations for State of Connecticut jobs (The

State provided a pension and health care benefits upon retirement after 10 years of service) during the late 90's; and finally landed one and started working for the State on October 8, 1999. It should also be noted that after my first "nervous breakdown" that occurred on the 4th of July in 1985, I had become extremely fearful of many things. I was afraid to go on vacations because I had my first breakdown after a disappointment in a relationship with a man I thought I had been in love with when he told me while in Acapulco, Mexico that we were "just friends" and my second one while on a trip to Nashville, Tennessee some time in 1993. I lost ALL self-confidence at that time except with regard to working my full time job and dressing fashionably. Working and doing a good job simply came naturally to me and I knew and always believed that I was good at working. However, I was terrified of driving to and working in Hartford and my new job with the state was in Hartford, CT. I knew I had to face that fear along with many others that I had developed since 1985. Things that I had no fear of in the past would now scare the living daylights out of me.

Ironically, unlike most people, I had no fear of public speaking and loved doing it in spite of all of my other fears. Most people would rather die than have to speak in public- but not me. Looking back I see that I had actually been in a clinical severe depression that I believe lasted almost 20 years. My depression was not your typical textbook depression. I still had my love of fashion and dressed impeccably well. I got up early and went to work every day, and I even went out on weekends to singles dances. Outwardly no one could see or fathom that I was depressed. However, I just never felt ok with myself. My passion for fashion never left me regardless of how I felt. However, I did become somewhat addicted to shopping for clothing and jewelry. Shopping and nurturing myself with beautiful clothes and jewelry was what I did to fill the void of loneliness, and the emptiness in my heart. My psychiatrist gave me drugs and kept telling me that I was the most well put together person he knew; but that was not enough because "I" didn't believe it. He said my problem was a chemical problem, medical and then I was labeled as being bipolar - a label I didn't take kindly to. I don't think anyone takes kindly to it because of the stigma and stereotypes attached to it. In fact, the label actually made me feel like I was crazy, and not normal. This label was just another thing to make me feel unlovable and to actually now fear myself because of the label. I had been kept on heavy enough doses of major tranquilizers to not be hospitalized but it came with the price tag of the loss of feelings. I had become like a robot...in fact remember how I referred to myself as C-3-P-0 from the movie Star Wars. I knew I had to heal myself and psychiatry was really not helping me at all. I wanted to feel whole again; to feel energy and passion. In fact, being labeled as bipolar seemed to just intensify my self-hatred and unworthiness by reinforcing in me the belief that I was crazy. In spite of this my interest in rekindling Clothes Encounters was stimulated after taking the workshop on the Art of Empowerment at Omega and I then created a workshop called *Balancing your Energy and Personality with Clothing and Colors* combining my learning from the workshop on empowerment, my spiritual studies about the Chakras and healing properties of color with my experience and training in clothing and colors. I loved Omega and still do. The energy at Omega is quite healing and I have taken other workshops there since that first one. I also take a day trip up there approximately once a year to experience the campus, the sanctuary and shop in their incredible bookstore.

In March 1998 I finally quit smoking. My mother who had undergone surgery for the removal of part of a lung due to cancer (she had only stopped smoking 6 years before getting the lung cancer) had told me quite emphatically that I had better stop smoking because I would not like having to go through what she was going through! It took me two years after her death to quit, but I finally quit on March 5, 1998. I had a medical scare and just quit cold turkey. I subsequently allowed myself to eat whatever I wanted to, substituting food for cigarettes and gained at least 30 pounds within the year. None of my form fitting clothes fit me and so I had to go out and buy new clothes. This was a perfect time for a new wardrobe because the New Age scene I had begun to become involved with sported loose fitting, free flowing clothing that is light and airy like spirit (the essence of the style of Indian clothing). I bought a few outfits that I began wearing and enjoyed the comfort of wearing them. I dressed them up with my accessories and added my personal touches to the relaxed styles. However, I felt that they did not "flatter my figure" and made me look fat and frumpy. So, I started going on diet after diet and I kept vacillating between wanting to wear form fitting clothing and free flowing clothes. I settled into what I now call "shape-shifting" wearing the styles that seemed to fit the situation I would find myself encountering and what I thought flattered my figure best. It was important for me at that time to feel comfortable so that I "fit in" with the environment I was going to be in. Sometimes I wore a formal structured suit, and sometimes I would wear a loose free flowing pantsuit or skirt set. I wanted to "connect" with the people, no matter what the situation. My weight continues to fluctuate depending on my feelings about myself - keeping me in a love/hate relationship with my body all the time. It falsely seemed that my happiness or rather lovability and self-esteem in any given moment was tied into how fat or skinny I happened to be at the time.

During the late 90's I had also heard about Reiki healing and wanted to be able to heal others. I was actually somewhat in denial of my own need for healing because I thought my "mental illness" was incurable, and attended first degree Reiki Training on October 4, 1997. I practiced with some friends who validated that they definitely felt the healing energy and benefited from it tremendously. I too felt the healing energy coming through as well. Reiki, in simple terms, is channeling healing energy from God, or the Universe, from the crown Chakra thru the heart chakra and out through the palms of the hands. Reiki practitioners are NOT doing the healing; they are simply channels for the healing energy. I did not have any physical ills at the time; just psychological ills as a result of the "nervous breakthroughs" which I later learned were actually clashes of my ego when faced with the spiritual challenge of Ego taking second place with spirit leading and the not knowing who I truly am. I didn't think that psychological problems could be totally healed because the doctors told me that my problem was chemical and could only be controlled with drugs, so I took my drugs and focused my energy on helping to heal others and the world in an effort to help with world peace. My interest and commitment to Reiki continued, so I took 2nd Degree Reiki Training on January 24, 1999. I felt very connected to life and my self-confidence seemed to be returning. I couldn't get enough spirituality - this seeking of spirit seemed to fill the void I had been experiencing in my life. I read just about every book on spirituality I could get my hands on that stimulated my interest.

Meanwhile, going to work for the State in the fall of 1999 proved to be both the best of times and the worst of times for me. The best of times because I was hired at an increase in pay of $15,000 a year more than what I was making in City government and I had to commute daily to Hartford, CT from Waterbury requiring that I get over my FEAR of driving to and in Hartford. In negotiating my salary I had neglected to take into account that I would be working 5 more hours a week and commuting

28 miles each way to work. A major financial error on my part! I had a great fear of getting lost and ending up in the undesirable neighborhoods of Hartford and not being able to find my way home. (No GPS back then). I also was committed to overcoming my fears at this point. I was also awestruck at having such access to the legislature and the State Capitol. Driving by the Capitol on my way to work every day was such a majestic experience with seeing the State's Capitol that is shaped like an old medieval castle. It was also around this time that I had come in contact with the Eightfold Path of Buddhism and noticed that a lot of the decor in the Capitol was in the shape of eight pointed shapes within a circle, which resonated within me. I was excited to actually learn how state government operates and I was able to attend some of the General Assembly's meetings. It was an exciting time for me because deep down since I was a child I had also wanted to work in government. Once again Clothes Encounters was put on the back burner while I concentrated on my new job. This turned out to be a good idea because between the extra hours of work every day and the 2 plus hours of commuting, I was exhausted and didn't have any time left over for Clothes Encounters of any kind!!

# CHAPTER 5

# *The 2000's*

I did very well for my first couple of years in state employment in spite of some difficulties with my immediate supervisor. I had never encountered being managed like this before, especially since I had been a Personnel/EEO Director in the past and always worked under very broad supervision or no supervision at all under the Chief Executive; not to mention that I am self employed in my own small business. I had difficulty with not being trusted to do the job without a watchdog. I made friends easily with many employees and one of my fellow managers, nicknamed me "binger" because of all the fashionable clothing and glitzy jewelry I consistently wore to work. Colleagues were always complimenting me on my outfits and asking me where I got them and how I am able to put them together. I always added a special touch to my suits and other professional outfits that seemed to be different than the status quo. I began mourning my business because of this hiatus to work with the State.

Then, while at work in Hartford on the day 9-11-2001 happened, we were all sent home. It was a terrifying experience and the empathy and compassion for the victims in the planes, towers, and DC was overwhelming. As government employees we were particularly frightened. I wanted to do more to help heal the planet and the United States. On October 20, 2001 I felt compelled to attend Advanced Reiki Training and received that initiation and certification. I also wanted more than ever to heal myself as well.

After the initial crisis of 9/11, the tension with my boss and I was increasing and it all came to a head some time in early spring of 2002 (I think I have the date right) when my boss and I disagreed on something. I was a very hard worker and very conscientious and took my job very seriously. I was upset so on my way to a meeting outside of the office that day, while driving in my car, I became overwhelmed and was crying and subsequently called my Human Resources representative and said something about what had happened and was sobbing and then said "I am not going back to work after the meeting and that I don't know what I am going to do", meaning that I might have to QUIT the job, nothing more. She apparently overreacted to this, apparently thinking I might do something violent and the next thing I knew I was out on Administrative Leave and had to see the state's psychiatrist for a "fit for duty" evaluation. I ended up out on paid Administrative Leave for a month. She (the psychiatrist) thought I needed a break while the state looked into the matter. My own psychiatrist had said that I was fine and there was no need for me to be out of work. I was out for a month. During that time I had a small part time job at the Blue Moon, a small New Age retail store in the Brass Mill Mall in Waterbury, and was able to work there part time during that month while on Administrative Leave. It was a paid Administrative Leave and health benefits and seniority stayed in place during this time. It was the Blue Moon owners and employees who saved me and helped me grow spiritually during this difficult time. They showed me unconditional love and support. This time spent working at the Blue Moon gave me more input on spirituality and various practices through their young 'new age' employees. My EGO had been shattered by my experience working for the state and I felt like I was slipping mentally big time. Never before had I had a problem at work. It was a big set back, yet hindsight tells me that my time during that month was necessary for my spiritual evolution. The young people at the Blue Moon looked up to me and called me "the goddess" and even today they still refer to me as "the goddess". They saw my divinity when I could not! It was indeed a portal to my continued awakening experience. It was another spiritual awakening opportunity that I wasn't aware of at the time. I had stopped working on Clothes Encounters because my travel time to and from work with the State made my days very long and I was exhausted at the end of the day. It was also very clear in state government that state employment was the priority and there were unpredictable times of mandatory overtime that might interfere with a business appointment. Prior to this 2002 problem event with my boss, in the summer of 2000 I had proved myself in my job, so the higher ups in my Department were supportive of me during the month out and I had to submit to another "fit for duty" evaluation with the state psychiatrist prior to coming back to work. This one I passed with flying colors. It really doesn't matter whose fault it was, because I view it as another call from spirit to learn more from the Blue Moon people. It was simply another step on the path to healing myself and waking up to the essence of who I am. It was a truly a blessing in disguise and I love that I am now aware of this blessing. This crisis turned out to be another opportunity to return to spirit...yes, another call from spirit. I had also been exposed to the Pagan religions and learned about Wiccan from the Blue Moon group and actually worked at and attended a Beltane Festival (a fertility ritual that takes place on May 1st each year with the May Pole- a symbol of masculine and feminine energies merging together) and got to attend and participate in the rituals. There was the breaking of bread and drinking wine as well as the ritual of jumping over the fire. I learned a lot about Christianity having actually adopting many of the Pagan rituals; i.e., bread and wine. I also learned that Christmas is celebrated around the same time as the Pagan celebration of the winter solstice that occurs when the days begin to get longer as a celebration of the return of light. In ancient times, humans often thought the end of the world was coming as the days after the summer solstice began to lose more and more light and so the when they noticed that light began to return around December 21$^{st}$, they celebrated. It is also my understanding that Jesus was not really born on December 25$^{th}$ and I have read and heard that the Christians used this date to celebrate the birth of Jesus because they were on a mission to convert the Pagans to Christianity and tying in the celebrations dates was a way to connect with them and convince the pagans to convert to Christianity with Jesus as the light of the world.

At some point during the early 2005 after 9/11 I decided to overcome my fear of traveling via train into New York City alone. I didn't fear the train; just going into the Big Apple alone was a fear of mine. This was a life long fear, not related at all to 9/11. I had never done it since the 1980's and since the 2000's were my decade to transcend the fears that the 80's brought to the surface, I decided to take the leap. My best friend from 8th grade's in-laws owned an apartment in Manhattan not far from Grand Central Station and we were able to use it for a weekend at no cost just before they put it on the market to be sold. This also, coincidentally was just before the Park Plaza Hotel's Palms Court was sold and discontinuing their "High Tea". My friend and I had always talked about spending a weekend together in NYC and doing "High Tea" at the Plaza, so we planned it accordingly and it occurred that year on April 15th...my actual birthday weekend. One of my brothers took me to the train station in Waterbury, and the adventure began. My friend met me at Grand Central Station with the fabulous greeting of a Calla Lily (my mother's favorite flower, a Gerbera Daisy, and a Rose). We walked to her in-laws apartment that was very close to Grand Central Station and settled in with a cup of tea. The apartment was on the first floor and there was a doorman. She and I were talking and laughing aloud when there was a knock at the door. I looked at her and said, "Oh my, are we making too much noise?" She said "no" and we opened the door and there was my oldest childhood friend/neighbor from Waterbury, Connecticut who now lives in Boston. It was a birthday surprise. She had taken the bus in from Boston and was visiting and staying with some of her other friends who live in New York City. She was spending the day us, and going to high tea with us. Each of the flowers represented one of us-the Calla Lily being for me, and my mom. We had agreed that we were going to wear hats to high tea so I had brought my favorite silver straw poor boy hat with a silver daisy on the side. When our friend from Boston arrived she advised us that she had been shopping at a cool store in the Village called "Brigitts" (my mother's first name was Brigida, after Saint Brigid, and remember it was my birthday.) We were also going to stop in at the Brigitt's store. We then proceeded to walk down 5th Avenue for a while because our reservation for high tea wasn't until 2:00pm so the three of us with our fabulous hats on went strolling down 5th!! We came upon St. Patrick's Cathedral on Fifth Avenue and I said that I had never been in that church, so we went in. They were searching pocketbooks for weapons as we entered the church (aftershocks of 9/11 I guess) and when they saw the three of us ladies with our chapeaus they waved us in without searching our bags. We felt very special and privileged, since everyone else had to open their purses and be searched. The City was still in a heightened state of fear and awareness even four years later. I looked around and saw that there were numerous areas where one could light candles when suddenly one of my friends said, "Dee Dee, do you want to light a candle for your mother?" I responded "yes" that was exactly my intent and I was looking for which section felt right to do it in. I then spontaneously walked to the left and found a little nook with candles and looked up at the statues and put my offering in the box, picked up a stick and proceeded to light a candle. When I looked up and saw the statue in front of me I noticed that it was "St. Brigid". I had no idea that there would be a statue of St. Brigid at the Cathedral and I had never seen a picture or statue of her before. I was shocked and then read the story about her on the side of the statue and it said that her feast day is February 1st. I then got the chills up and down my body because my mother died on February 1, 1996 and her name was Brigida! And that day was MY actual birthday. A superb acknowledgement and message from spirit! The signs are always appearing for everyone, however, we usually are so deep in thought and matter that we do not notice it. I am so grateful for this awareness.

The entire weekend in the Big Apple was a blast. We went to High Tea at the Park Plaza that afternoon, and then we walked down to Greenwich Village and SoHo too. It was my first time in the Village and SoHo. My other friend went to spend the rest of the weekend with another one of her friends and we went back to the apartment. The next day the two of us walked down to Ground Zero. It was very eerie and we met a street prophet and talked with him for a while. We learned from him that 9/11 was inevitable and he provided to us documents supporting that. We had a great time and I overcame my fear of taking the train into the Big Apple and a bonus of a visit from spirit at St. Patrick's Cathedral. A very productive fun filled weekend coupled with the meeting and overcoming a fear that had been bogging me down. I felt empowered.

While working in Hartford, (some time around 2002 or 2003) my cubicle had been relocated and I was placed next to a woman that I began to get to know and one day we were talking when the topic of spirituality came up (she was somewhat of a Wiccan practitioner). She also mentioned Shamanism and that I might want to find out what my "power animal" was. When I asked her how to find out, she told me about Keshav Howe, a Shaman in Glastonbury, Connecticut who owned a New Age store called "Two Eagles, Horse and Wolf", and that he offered workshops every Wednesday evening to discover your power animal. I didn't really know what a Shaman was at that time, other than having heard that they were the Medicine Men/Women of various Native American Tribes. The fee for the workshop was only $20 and I was curious, so I went the first Wednesday I had a chance to go and had my first experience with Shamanic Journeying. During that journey a monkey, an owl, and a pair of doves appeared to me, each with their own special message. The monkey reminded me to get back my sense of humor and to have fun again, the owl was going to help me develop wisdom, and the doves were going to help heal me from my loss of love as a result of the dissolving of a romantic relationship that had triggered the 1985 psychotic episode/nervous breakdown. The dove by far meant the most to me and continues to be my most dominant power animal. In fact, people actually have told me I look like a dove with my pure white hair and dark brown/green eyes!! I remember Keshav had told us that our power animal would show up in various forms when we least expect it and to try and pay attention when it does because it may have messages for us. Well, wouldn't you know, about a month or two after that discovery of my power animal (a pair of doves), I had to go over to the Governor's Office in the Capitol for a meeting. It was my first time in the Governor's office. The person I met with escorted me into a beautiful conference room with a couch and a coffee table that opened up into a conference table. There was an end table on one side of the couch with a one-piece pair of white porcelain doves on it. I noticed it immediately and commented on it telling her that doves were my power animals. It was a piece of the Angelina Collection (my mother's middle name was Angela-just a small connection). She asked about power animals and then she asked me if I would like to keep the doves and said that they had been looking for another home for them. I told her I would love to have them, and asked her to double check with the Governor to be sure it was ok to give them to me. She said she would check and did so. The next day she phoned me and told me the doves were mine and she brought them over to my office and gave them to me. They are in my living room in a place of honor on my bookshelf. I happen to believe that there are no such things as coincidences or accidents, but rather synchronicity and we need to be aware of it when it shows up in our lives. Awakening moments are here all the time for each one of us; it's just that not everyone is open or aware of them all the time. These doves were another confirmation that I was on the right path and that there was a true teacher in my midst. I didn't even know that I needed a teacher at this time, and working with Keshav on a regular basis did not happen until some time in 2004, after a huge crisis in my life regarding my job.

Things ran hot and cold with me at work and problems escalated between my boss and I, and some time in the spring of 2004 we had an argument that landed me out again on paid Administrative Leave this time only for 2 or 3 days. When I came back I was issued a verbal counseling, my very first ever in my lifetime of working. I knew then that I needed to get out of that situation, so I really started to apply for jobs at different state agencies. They weren't ever going to promote me at that Department and often times in state service you need to apply to different and larger state agencies in order to get promoted. I took all of the exams for promotion within my field of Affirmative Action and Equal Employment Opportunity and passed them with flying colors. I applied to a couple of openings and interviewed well for them, usually coming out in the top 2 candidates but losing out to the other person which in all cases happened to be minority women. It is a field that is heavily dominated by women and minorities and the competition is tough. After no success in getting hired into another agency, I finally accepted and surrendered to staying there and decided to rise above the small and petty things that were making me crazy. At some point during 2003 or 2004 after total frustration with my life and work I had driven myself to the psychiatric unit of one of our local hospitals and signed myself in. I spent 2 or 3 nights there, got stabilized and returned home and to work. However, I am not sure when I had the epiphany to go to Keshav Howe's, (the Shaman through whom I had learned what my power animal was), website and see if he could help me, but I seem to recall it was after the 2004 incident at work. Spirit has a way of letting us know when it needs attention and this was yet another wake up call for me from spirit. I have learned that when it is time to make a change and I don't recognize the need or take action to do it on my own, the universe will have a way of nudging me to take action. At this point, I had had it with everything and everyone. I was angry and terribly frightened with life and the troubles I was having on the job. I had never before actually had any large issues with working and I hated myself and everyone and everything. I was in deep despair. I thought I had lost my soul, and wanted to get it back. I knew that how I was feeling was not "who I am" at my core. Psychiatric therapy wasn't cutting it any more. In fact, it never did cut it. I knew deep down inside of me that I was not this terrible person I had been made to believe I was and that there was something more going on than a "chemical" problem with my brain. A review of Keshav's website lead me to noticing his

Soul Retrieval practice and I also learned that he worked one on one with people to help them. Then I phoned him and set up my first one on one appointment with him. We met, and he assured me that I hadn't lost my soul. One of the first questions I asked him was when his birthday was. He told me September 15, 1949, which happened to be the exact same birthday as my first spiritual teacher's (on Rudolf Steiner and Anthroposophy). I knew that this was not a coincidence and I realized that this was the man/teacher who was going to help me get over my fears and help me heal once and for all. I also knew that I needed to be careful NOT to fall in love with him, that the potential to recreate my past situation was great, and yet a challenge I needed to face. I also knew on some level that I needed to go back to Mexico to overcome the fear of traveling that had been the aftershocks of the trip of Acapulco with my former spiritual teacher.

Keshav and I met monthly after that as well as whenever I had an emergency attack of being overwhelmed. I also began attending his Friday evening workshops in Glastonbury, CT and bonded with some fellow travelers on the spiritual path. What I learned and realized was that I had developed a disconnection from nature and spirit. That was one of the missing links in my life. I had turned my back on spirit out of fear of having more nervous breakdowns and living in cities only perpetuated the disconnect with nature. During this time I did continue to take workshops at Omega in Rhinebeck, NY that helped me to somewhat reconnect physically and spiritually with nature as well as get away on mini weekend vacations. I also told Keshav that I had lost my passion for life and I wanted it back. In spite of my apparent well-hidden depression I still continued to dress impeccably in my high fashion, avant-garde style - and I shopped for more clothes and still made up my face and did my hair impeccably. I never lost my desire to be beautiful on the outside regardless of what was happening inside and fashion was what seemed to keep me together throughout all of the sadness and depression I had been experiencing and somewhat in denial about. It seems that my passion for fashion is what kept me grounded and alive. However, inside was another story. The image I was projecting was a powerful mask that hid the true essence of Diane. I even fooled myself into believing that all was well. However, on the inside I was in severe emotional pain. I was lonely and feeling unloved and looking for approval from everyone everywhere. I was also seeking approval from Keshav. I wanted everyone to love me and I tried to please everyone so I always put on a happy face. And truly, most of the time I was upbeat and happy. Yet, underneath it all, I thought that if I was beautiful and pleased everyone then they would love me - an impossible and unrealistic goal that set me up for failure. I wanted to be perfect! I still ask myself the question "What would I look like or be like if I were perfect?" Keshav helped me heal the pain and suffering I was experiencing using Shamanic and Plant Spirit Healing techniques. As my confidence began to grow, and I began surrendering and opening up to the "what is" that was going on in my life, I noticed that things started to open up for me. This surrendering is not the same thing as "giving up", but rather an acceptance and acknowledgement of the facts of what was happening. It was the beginning of my realization that I needed to stop thinking that I had the power to control anything or anyone. There was nothing I could do or say to make people love me. It truly was the beginning of the opening of my heart, which, I might add, requires the willingness to have it broken.

In May 2005 I obtained a huge promotion in state service to another department, a much larger department, which provided me with numerous opportunities to face my "victim" stories. This did not occur while I had been aggressively "trying" to get the job.

It happened when I simply went on the interview thinking that there was no chance in hell of my getting the job, and just went on the interview for practice. The interview went well, mostly because I was totally relaxed, and allowed spirit to come through with the responses to the questions asked. The very next day after the interview I received a call that the Commissioner wanted to meet me for another interview. I knew that when you were asked to come in and meet the Commissioner you were in the top candidates for the job. I went on the interview a few weeks later with the Commissioner and a few weeks later I was offered the job and accepted it. It was a very challenging job, to say the least. My studies with Keshav helped me to deal with the pressures of this new job, especially when he covered the works of Don Miguel Ruiz's book "The Four Agreements". These four agreements are:

1. Be Impeccable with your Word,
2. Don't take anything personally,
3. Don't Make Assumptions and
4. Always do your best.

This job gave me the perfect opportunity to practice in real life these four agreements. Carlos Castaneda might say that the job was the 'petty tyrant' I needed to have in my life to help me wake up. It was a great paying job, however, it came with many very challenging situations that, I understand, was why it paid so well. I finally had reached a financial earnings goal that would allow me to travel and lead the lifestyle I had dreamed of. Interestingly enough, it also provided me with the opportunity to delve deeper into the essence of Diane.

During this employment at which I stayed at until May 2011, I basically had no time to devote to my image consulting business. At the end of the day I was so emotionally and physically exhausted that I had no time or energy to do anything else other than cook dinner, occasionally meditate, and maintain somewhat of a social life. My work with Keshav became a huge priority in my life as I found myself inch by inch being better able to cope with whatever situation the job presented to me. There were lawsuits and investigations of complaints made against me by my staff and other employees as well as complying with the whims of various federal and state enforcement agencies and employees, laws and regulations governing equal employment opportunity and affirmative action. Through my work with Keshav I learned how to face whatever had been presented to me. And yes, there were moments of extreme fear, anger and frustration and I did make numerous threats to just quit the job; but I hung in there because I wanted to get my 10 years of state service in to earn my pension and life time health benefits and I was more than half way there. I also had been raised to not be a quitter and my Ego wanted me to leave on a high note rather than out of desperation, so I hung in there. Not only that, but I had made a commitment to the job that I was warned about before accepting it. I had to surrender to "what is" and face each situation as it presented itself and I had to learn how to STOP trying to control everything and everyone in my environment. It was a blow to my EGO to have complaints made against me. This was another opportunity for me to see beyond what I held as the "image" of Diane into the "essence" of Diane. I had been stuck in worrying about what others would think of me if I was seen as less than perfect. Quite humbling I might add, and I also learned how humility breeds character. My own arrogance at saying to myself, "how dare they file a complaint against me", was brought to the surface, allowing me to take a closer look at how much like everyone else I truly am. Please note that I never thought of myself as better than anyone else, in fact, I always felt inferior to everyone else and my striving for perfection was a way I thought I would be able to overcome my inadequacies. Underneath everything I still never felt good enough and thought if I was "beautiful, smart and nice" then I would be loved. The problem was I didn't truly love myself, and every perceived error I made in my life simply served to reinforce the feeling that I was not good enough.

Of course there was a financial benefit to taking on this new job -the added income from this promotion provided me with enough money to be able to go on Power Journeys with Keshav and the others I was studying with. The true benefit of it was that it also provided me with the opportunity to live my life as I had been learning to live -that is, in the "present" moment. I began to gain more self-confidence as time went on by accepting the various challenges the job presented as well as the one's Keshav presented to me. One time he challenged me to go to work for a week without wearing any make-up, jewelry or accessories-this I did with no problem. The end result of this was my feeling ok without the physical mask of make up and jewelry. Another time he challenged me to go to work wearing something I would never wear to work - in this instance I wore a red and black plaid work shirt (like male lumberjacks wear) with casual pants, no jewelry and no make up. It surprised people because I didn't look as impeccably dressed as they were used to seeing me, yet I was still impeccable in my work-shirt look. I also went to work without any make up on a few other times on my own just for the fun of it. I began breaking my routines little by little and by doing this I began breaking down the conditioning I had been brainwashed into by society that dictated either overtly or covertly who I was supposed to be and how I was supposed to look if I wanted love. The mask I had been wearing was beginning to fall apart along with a lot of old beliefs that are no longer true for me. The result of all of this was actually me dropping some of the "image" I held of myself and gaining more confidence in who I am without trying to keep up the false image I had been projecting out to the world and to myself. This was a very pleasant surprise. Keep in mind that I was one who took a shower, washed my hair and put on make up before I would even go to the gym. In fact, I recently learned that some of the women at the gym had nicknamed me "The Duchess" because of the way I always was so well put together (and overdressed, I might add for the gym). What a hoot!!! I had always used clothing and make up to give me confidence. And I am pretty sure that many women out there reading this do the same. Don't misunderstand what I am saying. Clothing and colors can and do play an amazing wonderful part in our healing – we just need to know how to apply them appropriately. Hopefully this work will guide you in how to use it for your own spiritual healing. This guidance will be covered later.

Wouldn't you love to just use clothing and colors because you have confidence to wear what you love and to simply have fun? It's time to bury the old paradigm of "dress for success". Along with the death of the "dress for success" mentality, a softer version of Diane began to emerge - the true essence was beginning to come forth. As the softer version of Diane began to emerge, feeling like a victim of circumstances was beginning to fall away little by little and my new mantra became "dress to express!" In early 2007 Keshav sponsored a "Power Journey" to Teotihuacan, Mexico. I knew that I needed to go on this particular journey in order to get over my fear of taking vacations out of the country, so I signed up for it and went on the trip. Not only that, but it was a perfect opportunity to face the even deeper fear of re-creating the breakdown I had (and blamed on) after my 1985 vacation to Acapulco, Mexico. I needed to go back to Mexico, and how ironic that I would be going with the Shaman whose birthday just happens to be the exact same birthday as the friend who broke my heart on the return trip that I had taken to Acapulco, Mexico back in 1985.

While I am basically physically fit and a little bit overweight, I am not a hiker and do not push myself physically. This trip involved substantial walking down the Avenue of the Dead and climbing 3 pyramids in a single day. The first day out I climbed the Pyramid of the Moon first with assistance from one of the travelers from Idaho, Cherise (who I met for the first time in the airport at Mexico City), my guardian angel, who carried my back pack and stayed with me all the way up and down the pyramid of the moon. I kept saying " I can't do this, I can't do this" and then all of a sudden I made it to the top. I did it. It was grueling and I was euphoric having reached the top. Once on top, I sat with Keshav on one side of me and Betty (another traveler) on the other side of me and we were holding hands, when all of a sudden an incredible "light show" appeared to me out in the distance and all around me. The mountains and all other physical objects disappeared into huge flashes of light and everything became pure bright white light. It was like a huge lightning show, without thunder and then the whole of the world became pure white light. I could not see any objects, people, mountains, etc. – only white light everywhere. I was literally "blinded by the light" yet had no fear about not being able to see objects either. This experience cannot be described adequately in words. No one else was experiencing this except me I soon learned. Keshav told me that I was actually seeing a glimpse of my divine true essence - pure spirit. He said the light was coming from me. The light is who/what I am. It was an awesome experience-a true gift, and while it was happening I was crying out in euphoric exaltation. Later that day we also climbed the Pyramid of the Sun and the light show happened again, only not quite as dramatic. A much smaller version of it had occurred. We also climbed the Temple of Quetzalcoatl that afternoon. I never would have believed that I could climb one pyramid that day, let alone 3, but I did it. I had successfully pushed myself beyond all my perceived limitations and dreams. It was very powerful to push myself beyond my limited beliefs that had held me back from so many experiences. Not only had I pushed through my fear of going to Mexico again, because of my experience of the loss of love in 1985 during my vacation in Acapulco, I had surpassed what I had believed to be some of my physical limitations. Later that year, in the fall I went on another Power Journey with Keshav and the group to Cusco, Sacred Valley and Machu Picchu, Peru. This journey was a bit more difficult in that I acquired altitude sickness and had to be given oxygen and then caught a terrible cold for most of the rest of the journey. However, the altitude sickness only kept me down for approximately one day. The cold didn't stop me at all from climbing the Incan remains at Machu Picchu. I found a deep connection to spirit during this journey because I was able to continue in spite of not feeling well. It was when we arrived at Machu Picchu that Keshav required me to not wear any make up one day. Apparently he recognized that I was still so very caught up in the "image" I held of myself and knew that I needed to break out of that mold that had been keeping me from truly experiencing my divine nature. At that time I still didn't see the connection because, after all, didn't every woman want to look beautiful? I went along with it anyway. Prior to that I would almost never allow myself to be seen in public without make up. Keshav continued to challenge me to experiment with not wearing make-up to work, and to dress in a way different than what I felt kept up my "image". I did what he asked and little by little I began to gain a confidence in myself that I had never had before. I was beginning to feel "ok" with Diane just as she is. Little by little my "beliefs" about who and what I am/was/ were collapsing and a new confidence was emerging. I had always dressed for "approval" in the past even though I simply adored fashion. I had used it as a tool to be liked and approved of...and the irony of it all was that my very "high fashion" dress was intimidating to people, men and women alike, and it only separated us even more, mostly because I was wearing a mask that was obviously read by all on a subconscious level. As true confidence in myself grew I noticed that I wore less and less makeup and wear very little to this day. I still dress impeccably, however, I am not as attached to "looking good" for or as defined by society. This was the beginning of Diane no longer using dressing to 'define me'; rather it is more like it now communicates and expresses the essence of who I am underneath. I was beginning to be more concerned with my dressing being in sync with my spirit and energy on any given day and being open to what life had to offer at that moment. I still do and always will love fashion and beauty. Beauty whether it is in nature or on our bodies seems to simply make people happy and helps us to return to our true nature, which is Love.

I remember a woman that worked in the same building as I did, whom I did not know other than to see at work, coming up to me and complimenting me on my outfit. She then went on to ask me "do you realize how uplifting it is for people to see you every day dressed so beautifully and colorful?" She went on to say that my outfits bring a smile to her face whenever she sees me. Now that's the impact I want to make with my dressing. I like to liken it to a walk through a park and seeing a beautiful garden of colorful flowers. They always put a smile on my face and make me feel better.

In February 2009 I went on a Power Journey to India with Keshav and a group of his other students. We visited Ramana Maharshi's Ashram in Tiruvannamalai...and climbed Mt. Arunachala and meditated in caves that Sri Ramana Maharshi lived in. During this trip my connection with spirit deepened in such a profound way that words cannot describe it. We spent a good deal of our time in India in complete silence, which helped me to delve more deeply into my core and to see that I really was not the image I had so desperately been trying to hang onto all of my life. There was an emptiness inside of me that surprisingly was full of bliss and joy at seeing this no-thingness. I truly realized that I am not the "thoughts" I had "thought" I was. Not the "good, the bad or the ugly". I cannot tell you who I am in terms that you would understand, but I can tell you I am not who or what you or I think I am or have thought I was. Who you are is a discovery and a journey you need to take alone, however, this point in my story seems like a good Segway into my program that I will cover more in depth shortly and can help you begin your own journey of discovery and perhaps circumvent some of the struggles that may come along the way. You will begin to learn how to wake up to the truth of who you are.

I continue attending Keshav's Friday evening workshops, and Power Journeys and I am a member of his Advanced Shamanic Group that meets once a month. I continue meeting with him one on one routinely as I continue going deeper down the rabbit hole, and experience the peeling away of the layers of my conditioning revealing the true essence of Diane's divinity. As time goes on I have many "aha" moments with the experience of seeing into the heart of just what is really happening and who I am. I have also learned how to use my body as a barometer for what is going on emotionally and spiritually with me. The depths of who we are have no bottom. The journey is endless and fun.

Specific to Clothes Encounters and this new program I have been working with, I developed the ability to know how to determine what colors and clothing style to wear on any given day to either enhance how I was feeling or to help uplift me on those low energy days that we all have. I learned how to work with clothing and colors through a new awareness of their true essence rather than only to the meanings we humans tend to attach to them. I even learned to use them in order to help me wind down when I was experiencing a lot of energy in the form of stress that needs to occasionally be tempered.

During my Apprenticeship with Keshav he introduced me to Chinese and Tibetan philosophies and medicine involving the 5 elements of: earth, fire, water, wood (or air), and metal. I learned that each one of our spirits is dominated by one of these elements as a "causative factor" of where we go in and out of balance. I learned that each of these elements and their causative factor are linked to two organs (called organ networks) in our human bodies and each organ network is influenced by all the others. An imbalance in one can and often does cause a reaction in the other. Since the skin is the largest organ (although not listed directly as one of the 5 organ networks) in the body that essentially holds our bodies together, it cannot help but be affected by the clothing and the colors of the clothing we are wearing simply because of the proximity of them to the skin. This influence is subtle (and while can help in healing, note that they can do NO harm), probably due to the fact that they sit on the surface of the skin and do not enter into the pores and vibrate at a much lower frequency than the sun, however they can and often do have an impact on us, particularly on how we "feel" since it, the clothing, actually touches the skin, impacting the sense of touch. In fact, researchers have performed studies on blind individuals by surrounding them in 4 walls of the color red monitoring their blood pressure immediately before and after while surrounded by the colors and the results were that the color red actually influenced their blood pressure by increasing it. With the color green their blood pressure lowered. It is not a tremendous variance, so one should not mistake clothing as a treatment for a problem with high or low blood pressure. The use of clothing and colors that I mention has to do with spiritual healing and is NOT to be considered as medical advice of any kind - and one should always get medicinal advice from a trained qualified medical professional. This may not equate to not wearing red if you have high blood pressure, I am simply sharing it as a bit of information to show that color can have a physiological impact on the human body...*Disclaimer: Note, that I am not a doctor, nor do I profess to be a doctor, and I am not prescribing medicine, but rather I work in the field of spiritual healing and my own experience of fashion's role in that healing.* It is logical to conclude that just like the sun on our skin provides us with essential Vitamin D, it makes sense that the clothing we wear can have an impact on our bodies as well. You can even do a color test to prove to yourself that we are physiologically impacted by colors. Try this if you are skeptical: Take a bright yellow color chip and place it on a clean, unlined piece of blank white paper. Stare at the chip without blinking for as long as you can and when it becomes uncomfortable to your eyes, move your focus to a side of the white paper and notice what happens. Notice what happens. What do you see?

STOP!...DO NOT READ AHEAD!..NOTICE WHAT YOU SEE, WHAT HAPPENS?......

ANSWER: No peeking until you have done the exercise: You will see that the image of the chip appears in some shade of violet or purple on the white paper. This is due to your overexposure to the color yellow. Violet/purple is the opposite or complementary color of yellow on the color wheel. Our bodies actually respond to the overexposure to the color yellow by visually creating the color purple, the opposite color of yellow, violet's complement, on the color wheel. You can readily see how this is a physiological response to the color. You can do this test with all the colors of the rainbow and depending on the intensity of the color and the length of the staring at it, the depth of color of its complement will appear in similar value and intensity. This is similar to what happens to us when we are driving at night and staring at oncoming traffic and headlights – notice when you look away from the lights you will see a darker version of the shape of the headlights which is purple, the opposite of the bright yellow headlights.

I have also been studying Chinese and Eastern Philosophy and the relationship of the five (5) elements and their respective organ networks to the human body and psyche. As a result of these studies I began to see a common thread emerging as to how the 5 elements relate to clothing and colors and style. I began to revisit my previous studies on clothing and colors and shifted the focus of their meanings to include the essence of them rather than only the outer projection of them. This happened as a result of my own journey down the rabbit hole to the discovery of Diane and learning my own relationship to the 5 elements. It seems to me that each of us has the simple purpose in life of discovering our true selves. What we want to do is get to the truth - and the truth is neither good nor bad...It simply is. I have been able to use clothing and colors to help balance my energy when I am out of balance. I learned how to let spirit guide me by monitoring my body signals of discomfort as a barometer for what my needs are. I also learned that when I am resistant to what is happening around me in life my body responds in a variety of ways: such as, a headache, a neck ache, heartburn, stomach upsets, gas or constipation. These body sensations are a signal for me to sit with the discomfort and ask spirit to guide me as to what therapy in the form of clothing and colors will assist me in facing the resistance. In many cases, I simply need help in opening up to what life is presenting and by wearing a color or style that is associated with that particular area of passion related to the discomfort often helps to tone down and understand the discomfort. What I am professing with using clothing and colors is to help heal what is going on with me on the spiritual level. I happen to believe that when we heal our spirits first, physical and emotional healings are then possible. As I mentioned before, I am not a doctor. Any prescriptions or healing remedies that I am advocating are for helping to heal on the spiritual level, which in turn can help us emotionally and physically. They are not cures, but rather help with healing on the spiritual level that ultimately can help you both emotionally and possibly physically. Often times when I find myself in a situation when I need to communicate or improve a relationship I will wear red, a color that I associate with the goddess Venus/Aphrodite and the element of Fire. However, I do avoid wearing red if I am angry. As you know, Venus is the Roman goddess of love, and our purpose on earth seems to be to simply love ourselves, everyone and life. I am not talking about what we conceptualize as Love, but rather true love that cannot even be described in words. It seems that the word "love" has become polluted and diluted. Love cannot be explained; it can only be experienced. However, I can give you a hint as to what is not love. Love does not try to control anything or anyone, love is not jealous, and it is not motivated by trying to manipulate anyone. We can use our clothing and colors to help heal our emotional imbalances as they occur and then we are better able to truly feel and express love.

When I feel the need to find the courage to take some kind of action with passion I will wear red. Red also helps me to communicate better as well as to help me in letting go of anything I may be holding onto. When I am in need of focusing more on tasks or if I become overwhelmed by chaos I will wear green. Green seems to help me get organized and more focused on what needs to be done. Green helps me plan and get things in order. I associate the color Green with the goddess Athena. When I feel that I am doing too much or resisting what is happening and trying too hard and need to be more relaxed and in flow I will wear blue or black. Resistance for me is a signal that I am fearful of something. Blue and black help to bring me back into the flow of life. I associate the color blue with the god Poseidon. I also noticed that when I am being overly critical of something or someone making judgments, this is a signal for me to look within for compassion for myself and the other and I will wear yellow to help with mustering up that compassion. When I need to nurture myself I will wear yellow, and I associate this with the goddess Demeter. When I just want to retreat into simply "being" I will wear white which I associate with the god Zeus. I will touch on this a bit more a little bit later.

Besides colors, style and fabrics of clothing can have an impact on healing, so I not only use the colors to shift my mood or emotions on any given day, but I combine the color(s) with the style/line and fabric of what I will wear on any given day to help me be in flow with life. Some of this practical guide will be repeated and more in depth as you go deeper into the rabbit hole with me in the pages that follow.

This program will also provide you with some tools to help you determine what color your spirit craves on any given day as well as how to combine your colors and styles to communicate your true essence. I also will outline later on an ideal wardrobe so that you will have the minimum wardrobe to help you communicate your true essence non-verbally. This ideal wardrobe can be a starting point for you to build your wardrobe to meet your every day needs. Of course much of this depends on your lifestyle as well as your career. Remember, dressing is an Art...however, it is an Art that everyone can learn how to master when you open to the freedom to experiment and have fun.

One of the things I noticed during my relationship with Clothes Encounters is that, at times, I had begun to forget my own advice to others in my first book, <u>Attitude by Design.</u> That advice was to make your work "play". I had begun to think of my business as something I had to do to only make money. I had forgotten how to play with it. I was taking life way too seriously and that seriousness was pushing away business as well as happiness, rather than enhancing it. This seriousness spilled over into my relationships with friends as well. Because my business was image consulting and heavily involved clothing, I also had forgotten that dressing on a daily basis for me used to be fun, because unfortunately it had evolved into my making a "job" of it-a "what 'should' I wear" rather than a "what do I feel like wearing" –usually a different and more fun choice. This knowledge helped me see how I was using clothing and color to control my environment and people rather than to enhance my relationships and promote peace, which, by the way, are directly related to how I am feeling about myself on any given day in any given moment. As I delved into the essence of Diane I began to see beneath the relative surface universal meanings and messages of clothing and colors into the truth about clothing and colors by delving into their true essence as they relate to me. What was revealed to me is the fact that clothing is a fabulous tool to assist us in balancing our own energy in any moment on any given day. They should be a fun tool, and I have returned to making my daily dressing "play", like playing with dolls, only now my body is the doll formation that I am dressing to meet any occasion or feeling that presents itself. Do you remember how much fun you had when you were a child playing dress-up with your mother's clothes, jewelry and shoes? Do you any of you remember having "color forms"? They were sturdy cardboard paper dolls with plastic stick-on clothes that you could dress up and change in numerous little outfits. I just loved them. Well, your clothes can and should be used today to nurture your spirit and help you cope with what you have to face for the day and to bring out your inner child innocence. Not only are they tools for you to communicate to others, they are also tools to aide in your own spiritual healing.

One of the prerequisites to delving into your divine essence is for you to learn about your own relationship to color and style as well as how the universe, that I refer to as ordinary reality, views them. We all have prejudices surrounding clothing and colors and knowing what these prejudices are can help heal our spirits. There are no bad colors. There are simply colors. The good and bad that we associate with different colors often times are based on a stored memory of what we were wearing when something that we perceived as negative or bad happened to us. We label the outfit as "bad luck" if something negative happened while wearing it; and we label it as "lucky" if we remember something positive that happened while we were wearing it. This is what I call the psychological or emotional impact of clothing and colors. I remember having bought a Burberry plaid skirt set made by Liz Claiborne and when I wore it for the very first time to a training I was attending, I had an extremely bad day in that outfit. From that point on I could not wear that outfit. Whenever I went to put it on, I took it off and back it went into the closet. I never wore it again and ended up donating it to the Goodwill Store. I had attached a meaning to this outfit that it was "bad luck". When we label an outfit good luck or bad luck we are assigning thought-based beliefs that simply are not true, and if we can get to what is underneath our relationship to a particular color or article of clothing and open to that negative belief we can heal the prejudice that mind has about that particular color and then we will be able to use that color for, or with inner peace. In my case the story about the training was what was preventing me from enjoying the outfit. The outfit had nothing to do with the story. I had to go into the emotions associated with the story and heal that. Once that was healed, then the outfit was not the bad guy! I learned this technique after donating the outfit. There was nothing wrong with the outfit. The ultimate result of healing our relationship with an article of clothing or a color will be the balancing of our formless nature (spirit) with form. This is what I often refer to as the Yin and Yang of clothing and colors. We are learning to lead with spirit rather than mind/EGO or form.

It's interesting that my studies in Shamanism and the work I have been doing on this program have made me question most of the learning I had studied in the area of clothing, colors and fashion – not because the studies weren't accurate based on thought and scientific research, but rather because they camouflaged and failed to take into consideration the expression and essence of spirit. What I discovered was the missing link in the world of fashion.... the failure to truly link spirit with form. In order to do this, it is imperative that we discover who we are at our core essence. It is then that we can more accurately apply the "yang" (form) of fashion to work in tandem with the "yin" (spirit); Yin should be leading Yang rather than Yang dictating to Yin. The fashion industry seems to be suggesting that we lead with Yang/form by pushing the latest trends on us rather than including the piece of the puzzle that links our own spirit to what they are designing. Don't misunderstand me, I appreciate that fashion designers often times are inspired by the signs of the times, however, it would seem that the designers could tap into spirit to help society out of the abyss we seem to be falling into. In other words, use their ART to be more pro-active in creating peace and harmony and freedom. In my opinion, ostracizing or making fun of people who do not wear the latest fads, is not a way to create peace and harmony. Magazines and other forms of media should promote embracing all the different styles available without referring to preferences, much like the news should be reported without any opinions. I would love to see more ethereal designs rather than the over done promoting of sex in clothing. These ethereal designs help us reconnect with our spirits and what is true and help us to bring people together.

The following is the foundation upon which Clothes Encounters was created. It is worth **repeating** here: I woke up one morning at 3:00 AM with the words flowing in my head. I immediately got up, and went down to my computer and wrote it down as follows:

Clothes Encounters Philosophy

World peace is a worthy and viable goal which I know each of us has in the back or front of our mind. And it all starts with each one of us... You do make a difference! When we feel good about ourselves, we in turn treat others better. When others are treated better, they in turn treat others better. It's a chain reaction. Looking good generates compliments, compliments raise self-esteem;

self esteem creates confidence;
confidence increases healthy communication;
healthy communication creates harmony;
harmony brings World Peace.

*(The intent behind my logo of the earth with a belt around it is bringing together the world through pulling yourself together with a belt and your clothing and accessories. I have recently colorized my logo with the colors of the 5 elements (wood/air, fire, earth, metal, and water).*

World Peace starts with each one of us as an individual. We tend to not think that little old me can have an impact on world peace. Think about it: can you remember a day when you were feeling down and perhaps a bit cranky, when all of a sudden someone either said something nice to you or gave you a compliment on what you were wearing? Didn't that compliment make you feel better instantly, and didn't that in turn make you just a little be more pleasant to be around? Be honest with yourself on this. Do you see how that has a trickle down or up effect? Clothing and colors is just one of ways that you and I can easily make an impact on the world peace movement.

# CHAPTER 6

# *The Big Picture*

I like to see how what I do with my life fits into the big picture, and it seems that the most important challenge that faces the human race is how to achieve "world peace". From my perspective, it starts with each one of us taking responsibility for our thoughts, feelings, beliefs and actions. Of course we don't always have the ability to directly control or have an impact on world peace in the way politicians do.

However, one thing that we do have immediate control over is how we dress. Have you ever asked yourself how the way you dress impacts your world? Do you make judgments about the way others dress? Do you use clothing and colors to separate you from others or to attract others to you? Do you have a favorite color, a favorite outfit or a favorite style of dress? How about this: have you ever asked yourself how certain colors make you feel? Have you ever looked at dressing as a powerful communication tool? Communication about who you are as well as how you feel on any given day? Taking the time to discover who you truly are and learning how to communicate that honestly with your clothing and colors can be the start of your taking responsibility for having an impact on world peace. I am not talking about dressing to please others, but rather to gain the true confidence that being true to yourself that can bring about a change in the way you value yourself which in turn ultimately impacts how you respond to and treat others and how they respond to you. Dressing in sync with your true essence is Art and Art in a simple and easily attainable form. And it's fun and creative with a fantastic sense of immediate gratification with a minimum of effort. And you can be taught how to do it spectacularly even if you do not think you have any sense of style. Just ask me how and follow the guidelines that are included simply as a framework to work with. They are not intended to pigeon hole you into new rules and beliefs. They are meant to help you open up to your true nature.

I repeat in different ways throughout this work my feelings about the various clothing and colors so that the reader has more than one exposure to the guidance and information so that while you are reading this work you are processing what you have read.

When feeling insecure, depressed, or even angry, I find that I can make a shift in my mood simply by changing what I am wearing. Some would say that this is a superficial way to deal with a superficial issue, but it works for me temporarily until I can do the inner work to get to the root of the issue. This continues to help me still today. The key is to be in sync with your energy level on any given day and to know what makes you feel good. It's similar to deciding what to wear based on the weather that day only you are taking your internal spiritual temperature rather than looking totally to the outside for your decision. Notice how sunshine after a rainy day often lifts your spirits. What the sunshine actually does is bring out the various colors of nature more vibrantly, thereby making us feel more energized as well as warming our bodies. There are numerous studies and books about how the body responds physiologically as well as psychologically to exposure to various colors and I invite you to explore them if you are inclined to want to know what "most" people think and feel about the rainbow colors based on the numerous studies that have been done. However, it is my intent to help you step out of the "box", so to speak, of the status quo and to discover how you feel about clothing and colors and for you to experience true freedom to recognize your divinity and express it with total confidence that you are in sync with nature and your true essence.

I like to think that we all have a purpose here in the world, and that purpose (if there is any purpose at all) quite simply is to just be ourselves (our true nature). Being ourselves simply means to me being in sync with our spirit, our true nature, to do what we love and nothing more complex than that. Fortunately for most of us, we have a lifetime to discover just who we are and there are many characters we meet along the path of our lifetimes that play a role in helping us to discover our true self. Nature is very colorful and so are we all aspects of our environment. We are exposed to all colors every day and we are impacted by colors subconsciously as well as consciously.

So, in this light it is important for us to have a knowledge and understanding of what our feelings are about each of the rainbow colors that actually are the colors in nature, and how each effects us based on our spirit, psyche and body.

I have always been fascinated by clothing and the way we women decorate and adorn our bodies. Why do we do it? What hidden messages are we communicating to ourselves and to others? Are there right or wrong messages that we are sending or are they just messages about the way we are feeling on any particular day? Should we try and control our messages to ourselves and to others? What are our intentions? How are they being received? How are they being communicated? Do they even matter? Other than protection from the environment and overexposure of our more sacred body parts what are the aesthetic benefits of our clothing? Or do we simply adorn our bodies just for entertainment purposes? Can the choices we make on what we are going to wear on any given day help us to feel better or cheer us up?

Since ancient times man has been adorning his body using clothing and color symbols to signify rank and social status. To that end it certainly had been used as a communication tool and it seems that this has continued into modern times. In spite of humanity's being 'more sophisticated and evolved' even today we use clothing and color to express rank as well as social status and to communicate. Look at the significance of the American Flag. red, white and blue: conveying the universally known messages of power (red), purity (white), and truth (blue) respectively!! Simply notice the way people dress in corporations and in high-powered government jobs. The business suit with a tie has been used to express a higher rank and more authority. Wear black and it conjures up pure authority. The red tie continues to express power and assertiveness. I have noticed of late that clothing and dressing have been co-opted by society and the fashion industry to signify rank, social status, and yes, even to motivate and brainwash us politically and socially, locking us into various beliefs and stereotypes. There are various fashion rules that are adhered to by many even today: i.e., wear white after Memorial Day and before Labor Day, the length of dresses, skirts, slacks as well as the length of our sleeves, styles and widths of ties, color of shirts, height and style of shoes, what to wear based on our age, etc. You name it and there is a rule about what to wear, whether it is what is "in style" or what is a "rule". However, the so called "rules" of clothing, colors and fashion today speak to mankind's left brain, or rational side and leave out the key ingredient "spirit, truth, essence" known as our right side. They fail to convey the true truth! In my opinion, the effect of the "rules" is to imprison us into a situation of conformity and of seeking approval from outside of ourselves. They are used to "control". While I agree that there are universal messages of colors similar to their representation in nature, what I feel the fashion industry and society miss the boat in taking into consideration the true essence of the person who is wearing the color or style. What I am referring to is our authentic self.

Haven't you ever admired something on someone else and felt that it looks great on him or her, but you could never "pull it off"? Essentially the "rules" are in my opinion a con game used to fool ourselves into believing we are someone or something that we are not; and fool others in order to manipulate them into siding with us on an issue, or into liking us or most importantly "approving of us" giving our EGO's more validation, power and control. Ask yourself this very important question: "Are you a victim of the fashion police?" Are you actually the fashion police of your own wardrobe? What if I were to tell you that there are no bad colors? There are just simply colors and that our energy changes often and often needs exposure to certain colors at different points in time. Also, tuning into what color your body and spirit needs at any point in time is not a "thought" process, but rather an intuitive or spiritual process requiring you to open to the essence of who you are and what your spirit needs or wants that day.

As I may have previously have mentioned, we don't have a lot of control of situations that occur in our lives, but one thing that we do always have immediate control over is how we dress on any given day. Dressing is a way for us to nurture ourselves and our spirit at any moment in time and to communicate that outwardly, non verbally; and the best news about this is that it is one of the things we can do for ourselves that truly doesn't hurt anyone else. People may not like what we are wearing, but in truth, what we wear does not hurt them in any way unless they choose to be offended or judgmental – which is truly their own stuff. When will we ever stop looking for approval from others and when will we ever stop judging others by our beliefs about them based on what they are wearing. Just think of all the "holy" moments you are missing simply because you are avoiding and judging someone negatively because of what they are wearing. Not to mention the other side of the coin, which is how many people are avoiding you because of their judgments of what you are wearing. Do you care what others think about what you are wearing? Are you willing to dress in the way that best expresses your true essence? Dare to wear your true heart's desire! I am not anti-fashion, in fact, I am extremely passionate about fashion and love that the fashion industry has now supplied us with an infinite number of styles and looks for us to choose from. The designers are on the right path to giving us more options to express our own divinity freely. My only criticism is when they try to lure us into wearing whatever they dictate to us as the "in" thing to wear and that everyone should have it with the underlying message that you are "no one" if you are not in style with the latest trends. It seems to only create separation and comparison among us rather than promoting harmony and the spirit of camaraderie and unity. The program outlined here is just the right medicine to help you select the colors and styles that you will use to adorn your precious body in sync with your spirit on each day.

Notice that I am referring to your body as being precious! This is because most of us either hate our bodies or take them for granted. For most of my life I have had a love/hate relationship with my body because I have always fought a winning and losing battle with my weight. Ever since Twiggy (who started modeling some time around 1966) I have been ashamed of my body. I nearly killed myself through starvation to attain the perfect body although I had never reached the stage of anorexia or bulimia. I grew up comparing myself physically to everyone else I met never feeling good enough or worthy of receiving love. I couldn't help but compare my body to those of models and mannequins. I seem to remember that somewhere along the line it became fashionable for women to portray straight lines to our bodies and that is a fact that goes totally against nature. Women on the whole are supposed to have curves. It is our nature to have curves! Curves are feminine. The Feminist movement that first appeared in the mid to late 1970's around the time that we women began to take our proper place in the working world and infiltrated occupations traditionally held by men compounded this continued hatred of our bodies, in my opinion. Make no mistake, I was and still am a huge proponent of the Women's Movement for Equal Rights and participated in it vehemently. However, I can see now that this attempt to achieve equal pay for equal work began when we started DRESSING like men, by way of denying the true expression of our feminine bodies. This did not come without consequences. It seemed a small sacrifice at that time; however, I seem to think in an odd way that it actually gave more power to the patriarchy that emerged with Christianity. It seems that we went so far as to deny our femininity in order to earn a living; we denied the goddess, the divine feminine. We tossed her aside and we joined in with the hierarchical management style dominated in the world of men. This dressing like men went along with the common concept at the time of "dressing for the next level of position you are striving for". In other words act as if you have already achieved it, and eventually you will. Once again, mind entering into trying to control our lives. I can remember buying a Navy Blue Suit and a White round collar blouse and wearing it with a bow tied around my neck underneath the collar. This bow was the women's version of the man's tie. Navy Blue was a classic conservative color. We adopted the symbol of Male (suit and tie) in order to "fit in" and to be taken seriously. Of course, what we were actually doing was dressing for the position that we were aspiring to achieve or hold but were not yet recognized with the same pay as our male counterparts. We were power dressing and it still happens today. The symbols are still pertinent and we need to learn how to use them without sacrificing our divine feminine goddess energy. (Today women still do not earn salaries commensurate with men's although much progress has been made in the earnings gap.) The symbolism attached to this suited outfit was that of a Professional or Executive/Administrator. Dress for success was the mantra back then. We wanted to be taken seriously and we meant business. We gave up our prints, dresses, lace and feminine pastel colors in an effort to FIT IN with the boys. This began to give us access to the Board Room and to be taken seriously. Women truly have come a long way. Just watch the AMC series "Mad Men" and you will see just how the workforce was back in the 50's, 60's and 70's. And you know what? It WORKED. While today we are still not on an even par with men, we have made some great strides to the boardrooms as well as in closing the wage gap between men and women. Are you beginning to see the power of clothing? My question for you to ponder now is: "What did women forfeit because of this?" You decide. My take on it can be read between the lines in what follows.

# CHAPTER 7

# *2004ish and beyond*

In spite of making career and economic strides, some time in 2004 I came to the realization that my life just wasn't working for me. I knew that it wasn't money that was going to make me happy. While I had been basically successful in my government work following all the rules, I felt that there was something huge missing in my life. I had been making okay money, buying clothes and jewelry and dressing impeccably in appropriate business attire incorporating high fashion accents, yet I felt like I still wasn't being true to who I am. In fact, in hindsight, I realize that I had lost or rather "sold out" my identity. These last few years I have come to ask myself what did I give up to make it in the business world? What part of who I am did I compromise? This crisis was the opportunity for me to seek out someone who could help me. (It should be pointed out that I had been working with a psychiatrist for 20 years and I still did not know who I was). In fact I felt like I had sold my soul for my job security. I felt like a prostitute. I was lost. I was angry and upset and totally frustrated that life wasn't working for me. I had lost touch with my spirit, which in terms of vocation was "Clothes Encounters". This was another wake up call for me from spirit. In desperation, as I may have mentioned previously, I sought out the help of a Shaman, (Keshav Howe) with whom I had taken a short evening workshop with about a year or so before. I had been feeling jealous of one of my good friends who was a recovering alcoholic and had AA meetings and affiliations with people to assist her in her spiritual journey. I found myself searching for my own tribe. I didn't quite "fit in" anywhere. I had good relationships with my brothers and sister in laws, however, I am single and they live in a couple's world and have their own friends and lives. Little did I know at the time that working with Keshav and others who worked with him would provide the support and connection that I had been searching for? I went to his website and noticed that one of his specialties was listed as "Soul Retrieval". When I read this, I decided that I needed to contact him to help me get my soul back. I don't quite remember just when this was, but it seems to have started some time in late 2003 or early 2004 as previously discussed. I remember that I was very angry and full of despair at that time and thought I had lost my soul. I made one appointment with him and thus I began a new journey into the discovery of who Diane is at the core. My own conscious journey down the rabbit hole truly began with my beginning to study with Keshav Howe, Spiritual Counselor & Shaman, Master Healer and Teacher. It has been a truly enlightening experience of learning how to open to life as it is and to connect with the essence of Diane. I became an Apprentice with Keshav and continue to study with him while writing this book, which in a funny way is a sequel to my first book "Attitude by Design". Through this study I realized that in some ways I had lost touch with my feminine side: the "Yin" of Diane, the divine feminine which we all have, both men and women alike, was buried somewhere under the facade of the "Yang" of Diane that I was projecting outwardly. Yang had been leading Yin, instead of Yin leading Yang. I had become pretty much identified with my masculine outer energy and had lost touch with my spirit, or feminine energy. I was all work and no real play. There was no balance in my life, nor was there balance in the way I was dressing. Even though my fashion and image consulting studies gave me the so-called facts about the meanings and messages of clothing and colors, I had been employing them on myself without being true to who I am. I was using them in a manipulative manner thinking that I would gain "approval and love" because of how I looked.

It's somewhat of a paradox that while my intention was to win approval, what was happening, in fact, was just the opposite-I was creating a distance between me and others. I was intimidating and alienating people because I now looked "unapproachable", like a model or celebrity. What is ironic is the fact, I didn't even know who I was and I didn't even know that I didn't know. What I realize now is that I had been using clothing and colors to try and fit in and gain approval and it backfired on me. Do not misunderstand this, there is DEFINITELY value in dressing for the occasion and fitting in – it's just that we need to take into consideration the "who" of who we truly are in deciding what to wear no matter where we are going. We need to be sure we are not simply dressing for the approval of other people at the sacrifice of our own true nature. In other words, we need to be in integrity with who we truly are that projects our authentic self.

During my apprenticeship with Keshav it gradually became apparent that a new Diane was evolving and it began to be projected in how I was dressing. The styles and lines I was becoming attracted to were different, and I discovered that I had reconnected with the divine feminine that I had been denying for most of my life. (Probably because I had been trying all my life to fit into a man's world with regard to having a career – a huge sacrifice I might add). I noticed that an inner calmness began to emerge when I was wearing soft flowing garments.

Once I realized that this is what was happening to me, I thought that perhaps many other women were experiencing the same crisis. I decided to turn my crisis into an opportunity to change the focus of my business and reach out to help other lost souls. However, this couldn't truly happen while I was working a full time job.

I feel it is now about time we reclaimed our feminine prowess/power by daring to dress the way we feel our very best at any given moment in time without denying who we are. It seems to me that we have lost our connection to spirit and this loss can be directly seen in the way we are dressing. It seems that the fashion industry, as creative as the designers are, are concentrating on designing clothing that promotes sex and staying within the material world of form to make money. We have become more casual in our clothing, even for formal affairs and we have lost some of the love of ourselves that looking and feeling glamorous provides. Just think back to how you felt about yourself when you dressed up in a gown or a tuxedo to attend an elegant affair. My experience of dressing up is that I feel like a goddess. I feel beautiful and divine. While the venue of the activity we are engaging in often dictates the style of dress, we still have the choice of dressing in a manner that makes us feel beautiful, like a god or goddess. We still have the choice to connect with spirit, our divinity. This holds true even in our athletic wear as well. This is not to say that we can never "let our hair down" so to speak. It is simply a suggestion that you can celebrate your divinity every day simply in the selection of the clothing you wear that day.

I remember being in the elevator at work one day during the early years of the 21st century and my supervisor asking me why I dressed up for work every day and she asked me how long it takes me to get ready. I told her that to me "every day is a celebration" and it is a joy for me to get dressed up and accessorize my outfits every day. I told her it only takes me one hour to shower, wash my hair, blow it dry, put on make up, iron my clothes and get dressed and accessorize. It's all part of the routine of my getting up in the morning and that it seems to me just that little bit of attention to detail and the way it makes me and others feel is all worth it. It is a celebration of life. Getting dressed in the morning is LIFE itself!

Before making a radical change in how you decide to approach your dressing I recommend that first you decide to begin to discover the truth of who we are at your core essence. It is now time to rediscover the divine feminine, not only in women's apparel, but also in men's apparel as well. Although this book is more directed to women's dressing, it can also apply to men and their relationship with spirit and feminine energy. The principles are the same regardless of our gender, so I ask that you view this with an open mind and heart and adapt it to the male counterparts in dressing.

It is the role of the feminine (yin) (spirit) to direct the masculine (yang) (form). Not only metaphorically but also practically. It is time for the divine feminine to make its return into the planet to take its appropriate place of inspiration. (Note: the root word of inspiration is 'in spirit'). Let's put the feminine back in feminism and be proud of it. By this I don't mean using our bodies for sexual exploitation, but rather as an expression of our inner beauty. Our bodies are our sacred vessels for our spirits and they are our primary mode of transportation. In truth, our bodies are Temples that hold our spirits and allow us to experience life and form on the planet. They need to be treated as Sacred Vessels and taken care of so that our spirit can experience joy and bliss rather than pain and suffering. This pain and suffering can be physical or mental. We should be using our clothing to nurture and heal our spirits and to communicate peace and love in the world. Our bodies are a tool or vehicle we use to fulfill our destiny here on the planet. It's a traveling machine! It needs to be taken care of even better than we maintain our automobiles. We need to take care of them and nurture them while we have the use of them during this short amazing lifetime on the earth in this particular body. I cannot emphasize this enough. Not only is it a tool for our work, it also is a tool for our play. Why not play dress up with our bodies and do it with the conscious awareness of our individual needs and inspiration on any given day without compromising the essence of our true nature.

Take the time to get in touch with your energy vibrations each day to determine what clothing and colors will either calm you down or ignite your passion, depending on your activities for the day and most importantly on your spiritual temperature that day. One of the most important parts involved in our dressing is to get in touch with our spirit, to know who we are and what our natural inclinations and tendencies are in life. It is my hope that this program will give you the tools to tap into that discovery along with the practical way to express it using your choices of clothing and colors. I sincerely hope that you will be able to identify with a specific divine archetype for the overall picture of your true essence, and to also discover what the clothing colors and symbols mean to you so that you can express your divinity no matter what function or role you are fulfilling at any moment in time. I have designed this program around the archetypes of 5 gods and 5 goddesses as they relate to the 5 elements of air/wood, fire, earth, metal and water that I feel reflect our true essence, and ask the reader to have an open mind and spirit and not be concerned with the gender of the archetype that most accurately reflects your true essence. Each of these archetypes, in my opinion, closely correlates to one of the 5 elements of: earth, fire, water, air/wood, and metal; hence the necessity to not get hung up on the gender god/goddess that best expresses your core essence. You will discover whether your core essence is more associated with: Athena, Demeter, Poseidon, Aphrodite/Venus, or Zeus. I used the Archetypes to simply help remind you of your divinity and to have FUN with this. While the tools provided for this discovery seem to be vague and simple, it should be noted that this process of discovery could take a day, a week, a month, a year, a decade or more; so be patient with yourself. You may need to work with some friends to assist you or consult with me during the process of this discovery. However, you should make it a fun and enchanting process, not full of mind streams, but rather full of openness to the guidance from spirit. In order to experience your divinity you will also need to spend time in stillness (silence) as a daily routine. For some of you it will be a challenging new habit. I suggest you start by practicing silence in short 5-minute intervals and gradually increase to 30-60 minutes daily. This will help you discover the vast bottomless void that you are in your essence. This is where the freedom is. Eventually you may be able to experience this vast freedom and love as you engage in your daily routines.

Through Clothes Encounters: 'Where Image Reflects the Truth', we are going to uncover the truth of who you are before we go into the actual know how in expressing that truth. This will require some energy, courage and effort on your part...some inner soul searching and a willingness to be open to what is revealed. In this program you will take a few journeys to your inner sanctuary to uncover the true you that has been hiding underneath the conditioning that you have fallen victim to from growing up in a society with rules dictated by fashion designers and other so called authorities– who simply read and follow the trends and signs of the times -of human behavior (i.e., during wartime camouflage prints are in, army green and khaki dominate the casual attire-reminding us that we are at war.) I am not judging the fashion designers because we all often get our inspiration from what is happening in the world around us. Essentially what you are going to experience is a falling away or dropping of the "image" you currently hold of yourself, which is actually now more than likely held as an *object* in consciousness that you have developed pretty much based on your parents, teachers, bosses, friends, and society, etc., and all based on fear rather than truth/love. You are not an object, and what you think about yourself is the image you hold about yourself which, in truth, is an illusion. You are much more than the thought or image you hold about yourself. Your thoughts about who you are are based on deeply ingrained beliefs that you hold about life and yourself. These beliefs are so ingrained and conditioned in you that you may not even be aware of what they are. They are beliefs that you acquired from your parents, teachers, employers, peers, politicians, actors and any other idols you have been influenced in throughout your life. It will take years of soul searching to peel away the layers of that conditioning, however, you can begin that process right now with getting into your core essence and you can use clothing and colors to assist you in the process. It is never too late because time is actually an illusion – it is always NOW. It is never yesterday or tomorrow. This should be a fun filled process that will open you up to the realization of the essence and beauty of who you really are.

One of the side benefits to playing with our clothing is that we can experiment with risk taking in life through taking risks with our clothing. By taking small risks with our clothing we can develop the confidence to take other risks in different areas of our lives: Things such as career choices, starting a business, choosing a mate and trusting our intuition in making decisions that affect us financially. In dressing ourselves, we can use the analogy of an artist's painting and how the value of the painting is based on how well it communicates the essence of the scene that it is trying to convey and how it inspires the viewer ....we need to dress so that our essence is coming through at any given point in time. Dare to Wear! Dare to color outside of the lines to make that statement without saying a word!!! Dare to express the truth of who you are or how you are feeling on any given day. Learn how to nurture your spirit while at the same time meet your outward non-verbal communication needs and obligations.

Did you know that "fashion" and "dressing" could be portals to unleashing your own stifled creativity? Through learning the hidden messages of clothing and colors that have become accepted as a part of our culture and your own beliefs and prejudices about clothing and colors that often are manifested you can begin to open to other possibilities that often open the doors to unleashing your creativity. This creativity only comes about when we are open and not hooked on our likes and dislikes and when we do not have a motive, desire or expectation of an outcome. Now you are more than likely saying something like "how can you say this when we all have been taught to set goals so that we can manifest them"? I have this to offer regarding that: "how can you be truly creative when you already have an expectation or desire for a particular outcome? These expectations and desires can only be based on ideas that are formulated by the mind and the mind can only remember the past or worry about the future based on past experiences. Thought will never be creative-it is always based on the past, a memory, or a fear based on a past experience. I might add, many of us have been kept stuck in many old belief patterns about who we are and the unfounded belief that we need the approval and acceptance of others. While it is appropriate to want to make others feel comfortable around us as soon as we meet them, we should not be attached to the wearing of something to obtain approval and acceptance. Balancing your energy and personality with your clothing and colors does require some introspection. We do need to balance being respectful for the situation as well as our own true nature when deciding what to wear so as to create comfort and harmony both within and without.

All of us have different relationships with various colors based on our experiences with them while growing up. This is what I call the psychological impact of clothing and colors. Regardless of how your outer body looks in a particular color, if your psyche is not in sync with that color that day because perhaps some time in the past you were bullied by someone who wore that color, you may either avoid wearing that color subconsciously, or when you wear it, have a "bad day", so to speak. It is important to know and understand your relationship with all of the colors of the rainbow, both externally and internally. Know your likes and dislikes and start from there. What I am proposing is to then go about healing your dislikes about clothing and colors so that you can take full advantage of the vast array of colors, styles, and fabrics that are available to you to help you balance your energy daily. (I will talk about how you can heal your color prejudices about colors later on in this work.)

Remember my story of my wearing an outfit by Liz Claiborne in a Burberry-like plaid to attend a workshop...without going into the entire story again, know that the day did not go well. It was a disaster of misunderstandings and huge anxiety for me. After that experience, no matter when I tried to put on that outfit again, I ended up taking it off and not wearing it. I had a definite negative psychological association with it. It ended up in the Goodwill bin, never to be worn again by me. It is also important to know and understand your own particular relationships with the various colors, patterns and styles. There was nothing wrong with that outfit. What was wrong was the meaning I had attached to that outfit that had absolutely nothing to do with the truth. It was the 'meaning' I had attached to it which is the illusion. That outfit did not create the havoc that happened that day; it had nothing to do with it. This is what I would call misdirected anger about what happened that day that I took out on the outfit. Now, isn't that pretty silly? I have since pretty much healed all of my negative associations with clothing and colors and I embrace all styles, lines, textures, and colors and use them to enhance my moods and assist with my energy daily. I do have preferences, likes and dislikes, however they are no longer attached to emotions. You too can heal your negative associations with clothing and colors and learn how to use them as tools to connect you to spirit and healthy communication. (I get into this more later on)

There are many more ways to use clothing and colors than simply to "project an image" to others. They can help us in organizing our daily lives. As I said earlier, we don't always have control over many things that occur in our lives, but we do have immediate control in what we will wear on any given day. I have noticed that keeping a neat and orderly appearance in my dress helps me to organize other aspects of my life as well. This spills over into organizing my closets and dresser drawers in an orderly fashion so that dressing doesn't become a major project that takes a lot of time. And of course, the outward non-verbal message of looking neat, clean and well put together is one of "she cares enough about herself to look neat and orderly, she'll be neat and orderly in her dealings with me". And don't underestimate the fact that "when you look good, you feel good". It can and does have a very profound effect on your own attitude.

For some of us who have hourglass figures (wider shoulders, smaller waists, broader hips) this means accentuating our curves, rather than covering them up with a straight line that makes one appear more masculine. This is what I sometimes call "going with the flow' of what God gave us. And even for those of us who have straight lines in our figures, we can add a belt or wear a jacket in a peplum style to help us create a more feminine accent to our figures.

With the majority of women, either single or married, going off to work every day our morning routine of getting ready should be a ritual we are proud of and enjoy, much like our Native American's brothers adorned themselves with paint and feathers before going off to hunt for the day's food. It is a way to honor your spirit. I, for one, allow myself as much time as I need to get ready by getting up an hour earlier than I would get up if I would have to rush to get ready. This is not something that I dread doing, but rather something that I treasure and do get into the moment with. Putting on our clothing and makeup and arranging our hair to greet the day should be done carefully and with thought about our goals and aspirations for that day in mind, along with the major inspiration from spirit. This would be what I call combining yin and yang to greet the day. More importantly we also need to take into strong consideration the way we feel (our mood du jour) when we get up to greet the day. Our clothing should be in sync with our spirit on any given day. Better yet, we should learn how our clothing and color choices on any given day could lift our spirits to help us meet the challenges of the day. We also need to know whom we will be meeting with or working with during the day in order that we may dress to feel prepared for the encounter(s) as well as to put those we will meet with at ease. We should do this for ourselves as well as for others. We not only want to choose colors and styles that are flattering to us and suit our mood du jour, we also want to be as appealing to others as possible. This is to help improve communication, not to build up our egos and not to win approval. Improve communication not only for the others we will encounter, but also for ourselves. Not an easy task but certainly one that can be managed with consciousness and tuning in to spirit on our part. We need to be in sync on all fronts. In other words, we need to balance the yin and yang to create wholeness. This does not need to be a major production. We only need to use just a little knowledge about the universal messages of clothing and colors and the insight into who we are and how we feel on a daily basis to dovetail our expression of our divine essence.

Clothes Encounters is my vehicle for helping to heal the planet. I have worked on healing myself for several years and have found that my choices of what to wear have had a profound effect on helping me discover my own divinity. By divinity I don't mean that we are gods or goddesses to be worshipped; but rather to discover the beauty and love and freedom that are at our core and to be able to feel it and express it non-verbally in what we wear. God is everywhere and in us too. God is not separate from us. In fact, it seems that because the presence of God is everywhere we often miss him/her because it is so obvious. And most of all, we miss seeing the God within ourselves. My discovery during this time has been that there are no rules and there is no secret ingredient to find freedom and love. Freedom and love are always here right now. It is so obvious that it seems esoteric. And we can use clothing and fashion to either free us or imprison us. Who are you? Are you the fashion police, afraid of the fashion police, or are you the free spirit that goes with the flow of life embracing life as it happens? Can you see beyond the illusion of what someone is wearing to the divine essence underneath? Can you observe without judgment? Is what you are wearing communicating your own divinity? Do you love yourself enough to express your divinity without guilt or comparison?

In order to have the self-esteem that creates true confidence we need to be in sync with the truth of who we are and we need to be able to combine that truth with the way we communicate with our clothing and colors.

From my perspective, the purpose of make-up and clothing or anything else we use to adorn or decorate our bodies is to add Light to the world by creating beauty, pleasure and comfort. We choose how we perceive them and can lift the vibrations and increase the energy in the world around us[1]. Clothes and other personal decorations such as jewelry and accessories are just like any other art form. One way to approach this is to view our bodies, from head to toe, much like an artist views a canvas. We can select our clothing and accessories for the day much like an artist decides what to paint on a canvas with the most emphasis on allowing spirit to direct our actions. I like to call this allowing spirit to direct "choiceless dressing". I know this is coming across as a paradox, however, when you open to this, you will see that in truth there are no choices when spirit is leading and there truly isn't any pressure in choosing the so called "right thing" to wear. That is to say, that there is no "I" or egoic image making the decision. We want to express the essence of who we are through the clothing and colors, much like an artist does with his/her subject on the canvas, be it a tree, a flower, a landscape, or a portrait. Another way to look at this is to greet the day making a collage with our clothing. Our bodies are the mannequins or foundation for our decorations. We can create the look of curves where they are missing by using a few common art techniques. Light brings an area forward or into focus and dark recedes or minimizes an area. We sometimes need both light and dark to create the illusions to give us the desired effect and feeling. Taking care with our appearance shows others that we care enough about them to care enough about ourselves. And especially on a job interview, having a neat and orderly, professional appearance gives the non-verbal message to the employer that you will take care of their business much like you take care of your own appearance. An impeccable appearance on a job interview is an absolute necessity that should not be underestimated. It is my opinion and experience that most employers know that people usually

---

[1]    Williamson, Marianne, "A Return to Love" Page 252

dress and look their very best on an interview, and once the job is secured, the employee becomes more lax in how they dress. So, remember, you never get a second chance to make a great first impression!

# CHAPTER 8

# *The Voice of Clothing and Colors*

So far you have been reading about my personal journey through life and the impact that fashion, clothing and colors, has had on my spiritual evolution and awakenings. I am now going to share with you more practical and how to information on my discovery of the role that clothing and colors can play in your life. So here goes:

Our clothing has structure or form. Straight lines with structure are more formal while curved unstructured lines are more informal or casual. My experience has been that when I am wearing straight lines with structure I tend to carry myself in a more professional, authoritative manner, and when I wear more loose and flowing clothing I tend to carry myself more casually and don't take myself quite so seriously. I am more open to accept life as it presents itself. The softer lines help break down the barriers to communication. They are less intimidating and invite interaction and communication.

Straight, formal lines tend to communicate more authority and make one less approachable. This can be somewhat of a paradox in the business world. On the one hand you want to appear knowledgeable and an expert in your field of work, yet often times dressing very formally in business can be intimidating to some people. The challenge is to know how to balance the two so that you are approachable, yet can be taken seriously and as a professional and expert in your field. This attitude is also projected outwardly and is seen and perceived this way by others as well. Believe it or not, you can still do all of this while being true to yourself. Quite the juggling act unless you learn how to go with the flow of the moment and one of the keys to this is to know your true essence. I have designed a workshop called "Reflections of Your True Image" to help people get a jumpstart on beginning this journey to the discovery of their true essence. This product is an attempt to assist you on beginning the journey, but it is only a substitute for actually attending the workshops in person. Getting to your divine essence and holding that consistently often takes some time (it has taken years for me)

I often wonder how we got ourselves in this predicament: The predicament of sacrificing our inner essence to "get something". I will make a feeble attempt at discussing my take on how this happened as follows:

It seems that in the United States we place a huge value on acquiring things and it takes money to acquire things. Our economy is based on competition and while competition in and of itself is not necessarily a "bad thing", when it spills over into competing for love and power, it can be very destructive. Yet, how can an economy based on competition spill over into love? It would seem to me that when one has a good sense of their divinity, it wouldn't matter whether or not they had the latest fashion or if they were the best dressed. There would be no competition for looking better than anyone else. There would simply be wearing what nurtures our spirit on any given day without any thought of looking better than anyone else or even being "in style" for that matter. Fashion for me is Art...a fun way to express myself and to bring light into the world. So how do we stop the competition? For me, it has been somewhat of an unlearning process (a gradual falling away) of first of all stopping comparing myself to others. I mean stopping it on all fronts: job, clothing, house, car, body, hair, etc. I will agree this is a lot to swallow, however, it doesn't mean giving up these objects, rather it means giving up your "attachment" to those objects and looking at the real purpose of those objects which is, dare I say, to be utilized to point you to your divinity which is another word for your "true nature". So the fashion industry like all other industry is in a "race" for the gold, so to speak. The "gold" being a combination of being the best as measured by having the most money for the best clothes. Success in this country has come to mean having more money, bigger houses, better cars, and better clothes. The goal being to be the very "Best" at whatever and this seems to be at any cost. We all have the archetype of the prostitute somewhere in our many facets; it's just a question as to where in our many facets each one of ours lies. In her book, *Sacred Contracts,* Caroline Myss guides us to determine the position of all of our archetypes and connects the process to the astrological signs. If you are intrigued by this, then I suggest you obtain a copy of her book and do the work to determine where each of your archetypes lie. It may provide you with some insight and guidance into the story of you.

There is another area that I feel has impacted the loss, or rather the 'forgetting' of our divine nature and I guess that is that somewhere along the line when models and mannequins took on a boyish straight thin figure concept. So what does this mean or matter anyway? To put it more simply, straight lines are more masculine or hard, while curved lines are more feminine or soft. Another way of saying it is that straight lines make one appear to have more authority while curved lines make us appear more approachable. When women began demanding equal rights and equal access to the boardroom, we began the strategy by first dressing like professional men. I am not sure if we realized how this change in the way we dressed impacted the way WE feel, but it did impact the way others perceived us. Do you see the powerful impact our choices of what to wear can and do have on how the world perceives us and how we perceive ourselves?

Depending on your role in any given situation you can choose whether or not to use straight or curved lines in your clothing. Of course, you can use a combination of different clothing colors, styles, textures, and lines to communicate non-verbally in a variety of fashions (pun intended). Just as important as the role you may be playing is the way you are feeling on any given day. You need to ask yourself what color, line and texture will give you the feeling of being able to fulfill that role and feel good about it at the same time.

You also need to be aware that we have been conditioned about how we should dress by the fashion industry and the media that communicates what's in or not in seasonally and the pace is very fast. These days pretty much all marketing seems to focus on the sensual and sexuality. It seems that sex sells and we are buying into it at the expense of masking our true essence and our innocence. This blocks our ability to directly experience each moment as it presents itself. By learning about the properties of clothing and colors you can become more aware of how you are projecting yourself to the world and how you want to look and feel in what you are wearing. It is good to learn what your conditioning is and how it came about. This is so we can allow the conditioning to fall away little by little as we get in touch with our true essence and develop the courage (heart) to communicate our true essence. (*Note: it is my understanding that the French word for Heart is their word for courage.*)

We all have different ways that we mask our divinity...ways that we hide behind our true greatness and hide our insecurities. One of the ways I have avoided the truth of who I am has been through my addiction to shopping. My mother often referred to me as a shopaholic and I lived for many years in strong denial of that addiction. It has been and is what I sometimes do to avoid looking within, to avoid the present moment. It is a way that I run away from my fears. It is a way that I avoid the present moment, always trying to find ways to get away from it. I have been so fearful at times yet not truly aware of what I was fearful. Rather than sit at home alone and sit in silence I would go shopping to pass the time away. This is commonly referred to as 'retail therapy'. I know I speak for many of you reading this. Finally, rather than asking the question "how can I find peace", and waiting for spirit to answer, I began asking the question "how do I avoid peace". Interestingly enough, by going shopping and spending money on things I do not need, I realized that I actually create more chaos in my life - different kinds of chaos like: not having the money to travel the way I'd like to, a house that is cluttered because of not having enough space in my house to store all of the clothing and trinkets that I don't really need. It should be pointed out also that there is a lot of guilt that is created while making these purchases. Working with Keshav has helped me to heal my addiction to shopping while fine-tuning my relationship with clothing and colors. It is my hope to help you heal whatever your relationship is with clothing and colors and to be able to use them to gain access to your divinity. I will go into some of the obvious and esoteric properties of clothing and colors and how to use them as a means to finding inner peace and healthy communication of harmony. I sometimes refer to this as the "Yin and Yang of Clothing and Colors".

# CHAPTER 9

# *The Yin and Yang of Clothing & Colors*

THE PROPERTIES OF CLOTHING: As a method of simplifying the properties of colors I have broken them down into categorizing them as Yin or Yang that will help the reader to balance their energy on any given day. These are simply my guidelines based on my experiences, and should not be misconstrued as rules to live by. Life is not always black and white; sometimes it is gray. This program will help you define what your experiences of clothing and colors are and map out what works for you. By Yin and Yang I refer to whether something is more masculine or more feminine in accordance with the commonly  known yin/yang symbol. Yin is feminine, and Yang is masculine. Another way of looking at it is that Yin is soft, and Yang is hard. Yin is receptive while Yang is proactive. Yin = approachable, Yang = authoritative.

Clothing is the container for the colors we are wearing and the shape of the clothing can either enhance or diminish the impact of the color on our bodies – impact the feelings to the bodies... clothing fabric gives color form and can be viewed as being yang when perceived as the "form" and yin when perceived as the essence of the particular style. Sometimes, depending on how it is used, yin is yang and yang is yin as mentioned above. Clothing as form allows us to experience the color in our physical bodies and absorb it into our spirit also having an impact on those who see it and their experience of you and the environment.

Clothing is made up of the following 4 major properties: color, texture, style, and line.

Of the 4 properties, color has the most influence on how we feel and how we are received and perceived by others. Much of the meanings that have been associated with colors are based on the colors associated with the elements: fire=red, water=blue, earth=yellow, air/wood=green, and metal=white. However, each of us is unique in that we have different relationships with colors at different points in time as well as with regard to our physiology. Our color responses are also heavily influenced by our experiences in childhood, adulthood and in our environments-I call these the psychological impact of colors.

## Color:

Color of objects is dependent on the different qualities of light being emitted onto them. Color has the characteristics of value, intensity and hue. Value is how light or dark a color is; intensity is how bright or dull a color is; and hue is whether it is warm or cool. Cool colors are yin and are inner directed while warm colors are yang and are outer directed. Light colors tend to be more yang and dark colors more yin. Bright colors are yang while dull colors are more yin.

Anyone who has seen a rainbow knows that there are 7 basic colors in the rainbow: red, orange, yellow, green, blue, indigo and violet. These seven colors can also be broken down into warm or cool colors: red orange and yellow are warm colors, blue indigo and violet are cool colors, and green tends to be neutral because it is a combination of yellow (yang) and blue (yin). Red, orange, and yellow are masculine in that they radiate outward; blue, indigo and violet are feminine in that they radiate inward; and green is neither masculine nor feminine. Each color has a complement that is often called its opposite on the color wheel: red-turquoise/green, orange-blue, yellow-violet, indigo-deep orange. Note that the masculine complement is feminine and the feminine complement is masculine. The sun is masculine and visible during the day and the moon is feminine and visible in the night. Get the picture?

Our bodies respond to colors physiologically as well as psychologically, and spiritually. If you didn't take the time to take this color test earlier, the following is another opportunity for you to experiment. To test your body's physiological response to color, simply take a small chip of paper in the brightest yellow you can find and place it on a plain unlined piece of white paper. Stare at the chip in good light without blinking your eyes for as long as you can without blinking and then look to the side of the chip but still on the white paper and notice what you see? **STOP AND NOTICE!**

(Answer: a violet chip appears on the paper next to the yellow one...what actually happened was that your body craved the opposite of the color yellow on the color wheel by creating the color violet, the complement to yellow-hence a physical response to an over exposure to the color yellow. You can have a response similar to this with an over exposure to any of the colors with the body craving its complement. The response takes different amounts of time based on the value, intensity and hue of the color you are testing. The brighter the color is the sooner the response occurs.

I recommend that you alternate your wardrobe daily so that you are exposing yourself to all of the colors of the rainbow regularly creating balance in your body and spirit weekly.

I do not feel it is any accident that there are 7 colors in the rainbow and 7 days in the week. Eastern philosophy and spirituality associate the 7 colors of the rainbow with the 7 energy centers of the body that are referred to as the Chakras.

These 7 Chakras are: Root chakra located at the base of the spine and represented by the color red; Sacral Chakra located in the vicinity of the sexual organs and represented by the color orange; Solar Plexus Chakra located in the vicinity of the stomach and represented by the color yellow; Heart Chakra located at the heart and represented by the color green – the center and balance between the masculine and feminine colors – it connects us to the softer places within us; Throat Chakra located at the throat and our speaking communication center and represented by the color blue; Third Eye (spiritual eye) Chakra located at the Brow area between the eyes and represented by the color Indigo; and the Crown Chakra located at the top of the head and represented by the color Violet connecting us to spirit. The universal messages of clothing and colors are also closely related to the 5 elements mentioned earlier as well as the 7 Chakra energy centers and often are used in facilitating spiritual healing associated with the Chakras. I will provide more on this later.

## Texture:

Texture is how smooth or rough a fabric is. My experience of texture on the yin/yang scale is that the rougher, matte (harder) textures are more (yang) masculine and the smoother, shinier (softer) textures are more (yin) feminine. My experience of natural fibers such as cotton, linen and silk is that they hold the energy of color better than synthetics. You will notice that most of our outdoor sportswear for things like hunting and horseback riding is more like cotton and hemp and casual and active like in nature while the softer and shiny fabrics like silk are more feminine and passive and used for more formal situations such as weddings, formal business events and other celebrations.

# Line:

Line in clothing tends to be either curvy or straight. Curvy lines are more feminine and straight lines are more masculine. When I feel the need to be in touch with my femininity I will choose clothing with more curvy lines rather than straight lines. In business, when I have felt the need to have more authority I would wear a suit with more straight lines and solid in color. Straight lines help me be more focused and task oriented, while curvy lines help me emit energy outwardly, be more people oriented as well as more open and creative. However, when in a networking situation for business I combine various masculine and feminine properties of clothing and colors in order to combine the messages of being a professional and approachable.

# Solids vs. Prints:

For me, wearing solids can also have the impact of making me feel and appear more focused. Prints tend to have the impact of scattering and emitting energy outwardly so when I seem to be in a state of being too focused or stuck, I will wear a small print to help scatter my energy. Prints also have impact depending on how bold or small the print is. Small prints indicate to me that someone is more approachable while large bold prints are more intimidating and dramatic. This can be further broken down into whether the prints are curvy (circles, paisleys, pastels, flowers) which makes them more feminine (yin) or angled (squares, stripes, brights) which makes them more masculine (yang). When I am more scattered and need to focus more on what I am doing or need to do I will wear solid colors rather than prints.

## Style:

Style for me simply relates to how formal or informal clothing is, and the environment of the social or business situation usually determines whether or not dressing for an event is more formal or informal. For me, casual, sporty or formal clothing can be either masculine or feminine, depending on the fabrics, colors and lines of the clothing. However, in the U.S. denim has become more acceptable for some business and somewhat formal affairs when combined with the right blouse, shirt or jacket. For men, of course, a tie with jeans along with a jacket simply creates a much more business feel than a sporty casual feel when worn without a tie or jacket.

Another aspect of style has to do with whether or not it projects a High or Low Authority. High Authority style tends to be more formal and Low Authority more casual. You can see this in the office environments of various corporations where the executives and administrators usually wear suits and the clerical support staff wears more casual wear such as skirts and blouses, shirts and pants and usually no jackets. As modern and sophisticated our society has become, we still dress in a way that signifies rank much like tribal nations of the past did with how they dressed.

## Creative vs. Fact Orientated Business:

There is yet another area to be discussed in the working environment arena with regard to style and that has to do with how creative the occupation is vs. how fact oriented it is. For example: an artist in the art department of a magazine will tend to dress in more free flowing, informal clothing to allow creativity to flow, and the account executive who is selling the advertising will dress more formally in a suit for work, and the chief financial officer of a company more than likely will dress more formally in suits and ties to express a more conservative approach to work. People expect you to be more formal when working with their money, and more open when in creative endeavors to allow spirit to lead. If I haven't mentioned this earlier, this can be seen clearly in the TV series "Mad Men" by observing the style of dress in the art department vs. the style in the finance and sales and account executive departments. Feeling confined in what you are wearing can stifle creativity much like too many rules imprison people and make them want to rebel. This is not to say that perhaps some people in more fact orientated businesses might be more at ease working while dressed casually. What I am talking about is more regarding the universal feelings of the symbolism of clothing and colors. Clearly, today, people are dressing more casually in business, and I am wondering if part of the failures of businesses might be attributed somewhat to the "casual" attitude of the workforce? This is simply a question. There is much to be said for working with some structure that helps us be more focused. Again, it is important to have balance.

I retired from the State of Connecticut Department of Transportation in May 2011 and have periodically been substitute teaching in the high schools. Times have changed a lot in inner city high schools from when I attended during the mid 1960's. The dress code when I went to school was definitely more formal than it is today. And I have noticed that the behavior of the students is definitely livelier today then when I went to high school. There seems to be less respect for authority today and I wonder if that in part could be due to the lack of structure in what the student's are wearing. It is simply a question on my part, not a conclusion. I am not a proponent of uniforms – in fact, I do not recommend them. What I do advise is flexibility within the framework of guidelines – mutually agreed upon. In other words, students should also be involved in establishing the dress code.

## Putting it all together:

Personally, I like to combine masculine and feminine energies most of the time in order to feel and present more wholeness in my experience of the day. You will notice that the yin/yang symbol is encompassed in a circle, which communicates wholeness. By studying and playing with the ideas in this workbook you too can have fun playing with your energy daily while at the same time meeting the needs of and fitting in with your environment that day.

It is important to be in touch with your own personal feelings about colors. I recommend that you sit with some soft instrumental meditation music along with the guided meditation in this package to help you determine your own relationship with colors and how they make you feel. In this way you will be better able to decide what colors to wear on any given day depending on how you are feeling that day. Take a Tip Toe Thru the Tulips journey daily (provided at the end of this work) to get in touch with your color selection for the day.

# FINISHING TOUCHES:

## Accessories (Details)

Accessories fulfill a wonderful purpose and often are ignored and overlooked when dressing because many do not know that they serve as a powerful aid to communication. I view accessories as the icing on the cake. In this capacity they serve as a tool to help direct the attention to our communication center, which is our face - eyes, ears and mouth. They also are a powerful tool to help us connect our clothing separates in a manner that makes the whole outfit flow with balance and grace. And, even more practical is the fact that they can be used to create more outfits out of separates which can be done by following the guidelines implied in the Clothing Capsule Concept following this section.

## The Importance of Cosmetics:

As you will recall, for years I wanted to be as beautiful as models and compared myself to them relentlessly. I never could measure up-I never saw myself as pretty enough. It was the same thing with my weight. Even when I was dangerously thin I saw myself as fat. If you compare yourself to models and movie star beauties you are setting yourself up for disappointments in how you look. (Note: rarely do you see movie stars and models stripped of their make up) However, we also do have the ability to make ourselves look and feel pretty by simply wearing a little bit of make up. Make up really plays an important role in how you look and feel as it relates to beauty. Wearing make up can be fun too. You can make yourself up to look exotic, simple, flawless, and/or alert. All you need is a little bit of know how and a few items of make up. It's like doing a painting only your face is the canvas.

The original Greek word "kosmeo" means to order, to harmonize. Taking this into consideration, then the purpose of Skin Care and Make up that we label as cosmetics would be to restore disturbed harmony. At the core of disharmony in the skin often times is a disharmony in the spirit or physical body. An holistic approach to cosmetics would take into consideration not only the physical aspects of the body, but also the psychological and spiritual aspects. So, when you choose a skin care routine and make up products, keep in mind that they are only a small piece of the puzzle.

I suggest that everyone wear at least 3 essential make up items daily: mascara, blush and lipstick. Don't underestimate the importance of following a good skin care routine. Skin that is properly cared for glows and to keep that glow you need to take care of it and moisturize it regularly. Drink lots of water too. Not only will it make you look better, it will help camouflage flaws. I also recommend a highlighter for under the eyes to camouflage the dark circles many of us have.

When using make up, follow these simple guidelines: dark recedes, light brings forward; shine brings into focus, matte minimizes. So if you have lots of lines on your eyelids and you wear eye shadow you should wear flat matte eye shadow, not frosted eye shadows. The same is true with blushes. If your cheeks have a lot of lines in them, be sure to use a more matte blusher than a frosted one and sometimes a cream blusher is better than a powder blusher. And remember, the older we get, the less make up we should use and that means eye makeup too! If your skin is beginning the get wrinkly on the eyelids be sure to use a matte/flat color eye shadow-avoid frosted eye shadows because the frost in the shadow will only draw more attention to the wrinkles. Dark circles under they eyes can be camouflaged using a soft concealer. Yin (dark) recedes to minimize, Yang (light/bright) shines and maximizes, highlights.

# More Tips on Career Dressing: formal/informal-authority-yang/approachable-yin

Remember, the more creative your position the more light and airy/casual the dressing can be. The more fact oriented your position, the more conservative your dress tends to be. There are many books written about the how to's of dressing for success and communication.... however, many of them do not incorporate "spirit" into them...it is my hope that with this program you will be better able to incorporate your spirit into how you dress in order that we create more "harmony" in the world. By harmony I mean inner and outer harmony. Be in touch with your own energy on any given day.... Work with the form for outer expression and the formless (your spirit) for inner peace.... I have learned that peace is not the absence of conflict, it is the absence of inner conflict... so ultimately, the clothing you wear needs to work for you, while at the same time assisting in healthy outward communication...

Speaking of peace, you may not realize it at this time, but understanding and working with clothing and colors can contribute to world peace. By learning about your own prejudices about clothing and colors and healing them, you begin to eliminate some criticism and judgments from your life. The end result of this often is more harmony in your relationships with others. This idea also spills over into the healing of Racism in the country, by simply transferring the misconceptions and prejudices we have about clothing and colors to the misconceptions and untruths we have about the different races and cultures that play out in Racism. There are no bad colors the same as there are no bad races. There are only our false thoughts and untrue beliefs and stereotypes that keep the conflicts going.

Here is another thought provoking realization you might consider: Can you see how the wars in the world are a macrocosm of the wars that go on within each one of us? Do you see how a change in one person can have a trickle down effect on the world? When I do my workshops on clothing and colors I often share this insight with the attendees in an effort to get them thinking about the global effect their core beliefs have. And yes, it can begin with simply learning about your feelings about clothing and colors that reflect your beliefs and overcoming those beliefs that you may find are not the truth for you anymore. In fact, I have come to see that all beliefs are lies – this is because I feel that if you have to 'believe' in something how then can it be the truth? In other words, if you have to believe something, then how can you actually 'know' it to be true? Something for you to ponder!

Using clothing and colors can be the first step you take in risk taking and standing up for truth. **Dare to wear!!!!** Give yourself the gift of freedom to express your feelings with the way you dress – what makes YOU feel good, rather than dressing for "approval" of others? This is not to negate that we also want to make others feel comfortable around us... There can be a happy balance in dressing for nurturing your own spirit and dressing to make others feel comfortable and for the occasion that is at hand. This book is about finding that balance and about coloring outside of the lines, about breaking the so called rules, and realizing that there are no rules except the ones that we agree to be a slave to. It's more like "truth and dare". Ask yourself if you are expressing your truth by daring to wear what makes you happy. Are you imitating someone else, or do you want to communicate and be your authentic self? Be just you, as well as a reflection of and connected to everyone else. If we were all supposed to look exactly the same we would not even notice each other. We would not know how to distinguish who is who.

For me the discovery of my authentic self actually began when I started asking myself the question: "Who really is dressing?" "Who Am I?" This conscious questioning didn't actually start until I had been working with Keshav for a couple of years. I had an "idea" of just who I was based on how I looked outwardly when looking in the mirror and yet how I was feeling inside, emotionally, was fearful most of the time. I was fearful of not being good enough either physically, psychologically or spiritually. I did use clothing and color to help me "snap out of it (the fear")! I had been conditioned by the media and what our Western society said I should look and feel like and guess what? I didn't fit into any of it...at least according to the little me that I refer to as mind or EGO. If you recall, my studies in fashion and image consulting brought me in touch with Eastern religions and the seven chakras and the colors associated with them. Along with that was also a noticing about how different the Indians (from India), in particular, were dressing. They were always in soft flowing colorful outfits. I also noticed that as the economy has shifted to a more global economy the Western designers have begun to introduce more styles that were more colorful, soft and flowing like the Indian culture. The influence of spirit was beginning to come to America.

Fashion is a huge tool in bridging the cultural gaps in much the same way that experimenting with various cultural foods does. Where East meets West is what I refer to as the yin and yang of clothing and colors. Have you ever noticed that the style of dress in India (the East) is very colorful, sheer, soft, light and free flowing? India is a culture dominated by spirit, the feminine, yet they usually express themselves in bright outer directed colors. It would seem to me that this is one of the ways of honoring the "yang" of life in their culture. I have been to India and it is such a vibrant colorful country. Notice the overall style of dress in the

West, particularly in the U. S. --much more structured, hard, and formal – masculine, yet very conservative overall in business. The most uplifting noticing that I had in India was how beautifully colorfully dressed the women from all the different castes were dressed. Even their fruit and vegetable stands were bright, colorful and inviting. Their Hindu Temples domes and gods are also multicolored and beautifully sculptured.

This Eastern influence is just the medicine the U.S. has needed to temper the hard-core competitive culture in the U.S. I feel it is helping us to be our own best selves, rather than trying to be better than everyone else. It is by realizing our own true nature, our own connection to the divine that resides within each of us, that we self-actualize and clothing and colors can be a huge contributor to self-actualization.

## How to use clothing for self-actualization –

What is self-actualization but quite simply the realization of who you are in your true essence? I also refer to this knowing as a knowing of your divinity, your true nature. For me it is transcending the "idea" that I have of myself to finding the true nature of Diane. I have "Dared to Wear" – by taking the risk to step out of my comfort zone with clothing and colors and to jump into the rabbit hole on the path of discovering, speaking and living the truth of who I am. I did this with the help of my spiritual teacher, Master Shaman Keshav Howe who has helped me and encouraged me to share my insights into my own divinity via fashion and image and Clothes Encounters.

Please remember as I mentioned at the beginning of this work, that it is difficult to keep this work in the pure chronological order of my life because my awakenings happened on different levels at different times. I have attempted to organize this work by decades and the reader needs to know that although I am talking in linear terms, my awakening is still happening in multiple levels of reality. In other words, life is not purely liner in my experience. Revisiting it now has put an entirely new dimension and understanding of it that wasn't noticed back then.

Sometime around April 2010 I began getting Elle Magazine and I noticed that they were showing what appeared to me to be a lot of chaotic mixing and matching different prints together in outfits. To me it communicated a feeling of utter chaos. When I looked at where the chaos was appearing in my own life, I realized that society is simply a reflection of what is going on inside of each one of us. This chaotic mixing of clothing was in my opinion representative of a sign of the time. Society is in flux, society and the world are in chaos. This seems to be the fallout of the decline of the American economy in 2008 and the fear and loss of confidence as a result of that was showing up in the fashion industry's designs. There was a loss of focus and harmony that the fashion industry communicated in the way that they were showing the newest designs. As I looked at my own chaos I realized that the economic crisis was an opportunity for me to look within and see what was really important. Ironically, I had a pretty secure good paying job with the State of Connecticut, however, I knew it was just about time for me to leave the job and put more effort into my passion-Clothes Encounters. The job with the State was creating a lot of chaos and unrest in my life and I decided that I needed to re-evaluate where I was at in my life and make some very important decisions. So, after I had my 11+ years of service in (2011) and I turned age 62, I went out on a limb and retired with less than 25% of my previous gross income between a small pension and social security. It took a lot of courage on my part to make this decision. However the trade off of being able to fulfill my dreams by devoting my full attention on Clothes

Encounters and my Holistic Image Consulting in what I truly consider to be my purpose in this life time, has been spiritually worth it. I now also have more time to sit in stillness and to open up to allow spirit guide me without anyone else looking over my shoulder. There are no others in a hierarchy to please, and no room for excuses either, I might add. People (family and friends) thought I was absolutely crazy to have given up such a "good job" with incredible benefits, yet I was able to stand up to them and stick to my guns under the pressure. I am no longer succumbing to the pressures of society, be it family or otherwise. I am totally committed to being true to who I am.

It has now been some 10 years that I have been studying with Keshav without any psychiatric episodes. The former label of "Bipolar" has totally fallen away. It wasn't who I was back in the mid 1980's and it's certainly not who I am now. The labels that society attaches to people can be more detrimental than the actual illnesses or dis-ease that we may be afflicted with and labeled during our life times. We need to be careful about the SPELLS we cast upon each other with the words we use to describe a person. Now I understand why spelling was so important in school!

What would YOU love to wear if you didn't care what other people thought about you? Are you willing to take a few risks with your clothing and color choices? Do you dare to wear what makes you happy and free?

Do you realize that what you are wearing truly is not hurting anyone? It is the "thought" or the meaning that you or another has attached to the clothing that is hurting or offending you or other people. Thoughts are actually nothing but thought forms that are illusions. They have no substance and no power in and of themselves unless we act on them. People are going to have opinions about everything including clothing and colors. That is how we have been conditioned by our cultures and society. As a society we have come to some agreements about what is casual and formal attire and when and to what events to wear them. There is nothing wrong with this, and it is respectful to wear clothing that is appropriate for the occasion. Within that framework of the event it is nice to experiment and have fun with our clothing. Ask yourself this question: "What if the earth is simply a playground for spirit to have fun with form? One absolutely creative way to play in form is with our choices in clothing and the colors. I like to look at life as a huge stage, a play in which I am playing different roles and wear different costumes based on the role I am currently playing taking care to remember who I truly am underneath the costume. The Hindu's often refer to life on this planet as "Leela" – meaning a play. I like to carry or wear a "totem" that I can refer to take me back to the essence of the true Diane so that I don't get too caught up with identifying too strongly with the role I am playing. It is important to know when you are dreaming and when you are not so that you can return to life on the planet. Regardless of which role you are playing, make sure you have a totem on you that will take you back to the essence of the truth of who you are so that you don't get caught up in and identify too strongly in the role that you are playing if it is not in sync with your true essence. The movie "Inception" articulates this perfectly.

I have also noticed that depending on what career I am involved in I have used the clothing pertinent to that career in an effort to "fit in". Oftentimes, I did this at the expense of a loss of my true identity. Again, there is a balance to be achieved in respecting others and the event and being true to oneself.

Are you beginning to see that Clothing and Colors can be the portal to freedom?

## Another take on Career Dressing – truth or playing a role?

Did you pick your career based on the clothing you are comfortable wearing, or do you wear your clothing based on the guidelines for the career you have chosen? What defines you? Ask yourself how you can adapt your wardrobe at work to be in integrity with your spirit, while at the same time being in sync with the role you are playing in your career. For me, one of my jobs was at the level of Director, which was the highest position in that career series, and the organization that I worked in was predominantly male and formal. All executives wore suits. When I first started there I pretty much complied with the status quo and wore suits most of the time. However, they weren't in sync with my spirit so as I became more comfortable in the job and confident in spirit I gradually made a few changes. I bought a few long more fluid skirts and combined them with semi-structured jackets to allow a more creative flowing spirit to come through. As I did this, my creativity began to soar much better than when in structured formal suits. I saved the suits for when I needed to make presentations to an audience that may have doubted the authority of what I was discussing. The suits also had the impact of making me feel more confident and gave that feeling off to the audiences as well. I call this a "win/win" so to speak.

At times I have had to dress in a suit for important business and do this out of respect for the people I will be meeting with. The universal message of a business suit is generally that of "power in the form of expertise", yet ironically, while this projects out to others my "power" as they define it, in truth, it fails to portray my divine essence that is where my true power is. In order to balance this I often accent my suit with a soft accessory such as a flower fabric pin or a print scarf (do you see the yin and yang at work here?) It seems that the impact of a power suit can be to become more aggressive, rather than coming from a place of stillness. Of course, when one knows how to use other characteristics of clothing and colors, one can soften or harden the impact of what one is wearing. This program has the intent of teaching how to use clothing and colors to help heal our self first and ultimately it having a trickle down effect in helping to heal the planet.

I have had a dual career for most of my life. I remember fondly that as a child I played with color forms dolls...what I loved the most about it was the way I could change the dolls outfits licitly split. Interestingly enough from a very young age I also had a dream of working in government in the area of social work. I remember a time while walking in downtown Waterbury, Connecticut with my mother passing by City Hall - a grandiose building with a huge bird bath in the front - and telling my mother "I am going to work in that building some day.", and you know what, I did. By the way, I was approximately 5 years old when that statement occurred.

My dual careers ironically embraced balance in my life: Yin = fashion, Yang=work in government. However, most of my life was spent working full time in yang (government) and part time in yin (fashion); and now yin has emerged as my dominant career path.

For me, I noticed that the 1980s were the beginning of the latest fashions getting more eclectic and more available to the average person regardless of income or social status...The 1990s was a time that women became more powerful in business and suits became more the rule for business. In the 2000's fashion freedom begins to explode and designer knock offs become more prevalent and available. This is wonderful fashion news for us today. Because of the knockoffs just about all the latest styles and trends are accessible to everyone regardless of income.

# Clothing in sync with your daily energy:

Have you ever noticed that some days you just don't know what to wear that day? On top of that, you may not have enough time or energy to spend time in putting together a nice outfit to wear. When that happens, do you take the time to look inside at what's eating you? Are you reacting to something emotionally? Where is the sensation of unrest in your body? If you can identify the location and inquire into it you might get a clue as to what you can wear to help you feel better...i.e., when I am having difficulties with people overstepping my boundaries, I usually feel it in my stomach and the color for that chakra is yellow (earth element) – so I try and wear something yellow that day. It usually helps me see where I need to take some action and give me courage in communicating better to let individuals know when they have crossed the line with me. It is interesting how we intuitively know how to dress in lightweight pastel colors when it is hot (summer) outside, and heavy weight darker colors when it is cold (winter) to hold our energy in. What we need to do is to learn how to tap into our emotions and feelings on any given day and determine what clothing and colors will help us meet those needs on that day. While the tips in this book are intended to give you some of the universal messages of clothing and colors that have been described throughout many decades, what colors and styles will assist you in meeting your emotional needs on any given day will depend on each of you individually, and you will need to do some internal work to discover your own relationship to clothing and colors. Remember that some of this is based on our past experiences in life and some of it is entirely based on our individual spirits. While we are all one and part of the entire universe, we each have an important role and that is to discover and be who we are at our true essence.

I have many clothes encounters stories in my personal life to share. One that comes to mind is when I was in love with a man during the late 80's. I stalked him somewhat on the weekends. We were friends and a bunch of us hung out together, and he and I indulged in some sexual romance, but it never went anywhere. I always tried to impress him with my clothes. I thought if I looked sexy enough for him then he would love me. One night I had worn an unstructured gauzy outfit (late 80's or early 90's) to Happy Hour at a nightclub in Waterbury where a bunch of us hung out on Friday nights after work. He told me that I looked fat and that I must have gained weight!! I was devastated and felt totally uncomfortable for the rest of the Happy Hour, I had used his criticism to "define" me rather than "inform" me. In truth, his comment simply was informing me that that particular outfit made me look heavier than others make me look. So What? So, before going out later on that night to a different nightclub I went home and changed my clothes into a sexy tube top and tight pants. I felt better, however, I saw him later, but he said nothing. I am pretty sure I never wore that gauzy outfit again and I cannot even remember what it looked like.

As I mentioned before, I often wore hats and headbands and scarves on my head. As I ventured into the cosmetic industry I morphed into dressing very high fashion and acquired a vast collection of cool and expensive hats that I often wore daily. Oddly enough, at the time I wore them to give me confidence, and the message it communicated to others was that I was extremely confident (Little did they know I was scared to death of not being good enough). Today I can honesty tell you that when I wear a hat I truly have the confidence to wear it, rather than wearing them to give me confidence.

However it is important to know that clothing may communicate different messages to others. Dressing very high fashion made me appear unapproachable because they were fashions that models wore while modeling, and people idolize models and generally are intimidated by them. This intimidation is actually a result of their own insecurities and feelings of unworthiness. So I gave off the image of being a celebrity and unapproachable, when in fact I was just trying to get approval. Funny how seeking approval in this manner only pushes it and people further away. What was an expression of my own insecurities was having the opposite effect on the way others perceived me. Women said things like "Oh I love what you are wearing, but I could never wear that...you have the confidence and security that you can wear that, I could never pull that off!" What I found myself doing was actually using clothing and colors and the way I dressed to manipulate various situations, rather than as an expression of the truth of Diane. I used them to give me confidence and while to some extent it is true that when you look good you feel good, it isn't the whole enchilada as the saying goes. Back then it wasn't true confidence, only impermanent, in the moment confidence that really did nothing to develop true self-esteem. However, it is a piece of the puzzle that should not be ignored because it can and does help guide one to develop more true self confidence. It has helped me with my insecurities many times, even if just temporarily. For me, my body is like a canvas and depending upon how I dress it, can make me look like a work of art that can either attract or repel others as well as myself. Just think about how good it feels to see beauty such as a garden in nature. Don't you just love to look at it, take in its beauty, and allow it to have its impact on you? This can be the impact that you have on people you meet on a regular basis. I am going to repeat something that a person who worked in the same building as I once did said to me one day "I just love how you dress. Do you know the impact your sense of style and the way you look has on other people? Your clothing brightens my day every day, and I look forward to seeing what you are wearing every day." Now that's a true compliment that made my day. Can you see how there is a chain reaction and a connection with looking good and feeling good? I remember the first time I went to a convention of Image Consultants who were affiliated with Karla Jordan Kollections' jewelry. They were all dressed in bright beautiful colors. It felt like I was approaching a beautiful garden of wispy flowers in all colors, varieties and shapes. It was an overwhelming experience of beauty and set the stage for a wonderful convention.

It seems to me that since 9/11 the world has been in utter chaos and the fashion industry seems to also be communicating that chaos to some degree. Now, make no mistake, fashion is my passion! However, it is my feeling that we can use fashion to redirect our minds into creating harmony in the world. We can do this simply by getting to know our own divine essence by answering 'Absolum' question to Alice "Who Are You" and learning how to become "Alice at Last!" (I highly recommend you watch the 2010 Disney Movie "Alice in Wonderland") We can take this journey down the rabbit hole using fashion to get to our "wonderland or underland" as the case might be. I have journeyed through my life wearing the various masks of what clothing was in style at the time – I compared myself to movie stars, models, and mannequins always striving to be perfect because as I mentioned so many times before, I thought if I was beautiful enough on the outside then people would love me. All of this was at the expense of losing sight of who I truly am. I was looking at life through the filter of who I thought I "SHOULD HAVE BEEN",

We tragically lost a very talented musician recently who sang what was for me the greatest love song of all time: Whitney Houston's "The Greatest Love" which simply is learning to love yourself, the greatest love of all!! When we love ourselves, truly love ourselves, there is no anger, no jealousy, no hatred, etc. towards anyone else. There is no desire to be anyone or anything other than who you are. Why you might ask? It is simply because we are all mirrors reflecting what's going on inside of us out onto other people, places and things. When we love ourselves we are at peace and so is our world and all of the people places and thinks in it. Loving ourselves is what allows us to truly experience love of another and love of life.

I can honestly say that until recently I hated my body. I thought I had a weight problem always thinking that I was too fat. I thought I was fat even when I was extremely thin. I gauged my self worth by numbers on the scale and even when they were the "right" numbers I still hated my body. I still did not feel good enough. Even though people always said that clothes looked great on me something was missing. I lacked true self-confidence that cannot be given to you from your clothes or from anyone else, but rather from knowing just who you are and how to dress expressing that. Don't misunderstand me, wearing clothing that makes you happy and expresses your true essence can and does impact how you feel – it is one notch on the belt that should be taken into account and often is overlooked. *It can be the beginning point*. You can and should use clothing and colors to enrich your spirit and improve your attitude. Where do you start? That depends on you. If you find your life is chaotic, you can take a tiny step to create some order out of the chaos with your clothing. This can simply begin by organizing your closet and taking an inventory of what you already have. I suggest that you begin this process with trying on your current clothing in your closet and discarding anything that no longer fits you. Next, separate the clothing into tops, jackets, slacks and skirts and place each group in rainbow order: red, orange, yellow, green, blue, navy/indigo, and violet, and neutrals of black, white, gray and beige.

Next step: you also will need to learn how to accessorize and combine outfits, and more importantly learn your prejudices around colors, and finally at the crux of the matter you will need to learn how to tap into your spirit to determine how you are feeling that day, and how to choose what colors and/or clothing line or style will help to nurture, express or heal that feeling.

This will depend on where you are at physically, emotionally and spiritually on that day. What I feel is very important is to have all the colors of the rainbow along with black, white, brown, gray, available in your wardrobe as well as a representation of the various lines (structured or unstructured) in your wardrobe so that you can combine the energies of these articles of clothing to help you nurture your spirit meet and balance your needs on any given day.

We need to also keep in mind that we are always being bombarded by the media and the fashion industry to go along with and continue the conditioning of society and the world. It can be difficult to really stay true to our true natures and dress according to our spirit, not according to the "so called 'experts'". Although fashion does go along with many worldly trends such as bringing in camouflage prints during times of war, in my opinion this simply suggests and perpetuates more war. I am also of the opinion that when we go against war we actually do nothing to stop it, in fact, we just give war more power! Just look at the four (4) times I have used the word "war" in the last few sentences. Doesn't it keep you in the thoughts of "war"?

Ironically, we need to become 'spiritual' warriors in order to transcend our conditioning and stay true to our true nature and create peace in the world. This brings to mind a client of mine who only wore beige. She expressed to me that she was actually afraid to be seen, and after attending one of my workshops on the "Yin and Yang of Clothing and Colors" asked me to take her shopping for a dress to wear to her son's upcoming wedding. We went to the Mall and I immediately spotted a pastel small polka dotted dress with a black background that had a slight flair at the bottom. Her first reaction to the dress was "I would never wear that!" I asked her to humor me and please try it on, so she tried it on. When she looked in the mirror with the dress on she lit up like a shining star, twirled around, and fell in love with the dress and how she looked and "felt" in it. She bought it along with a few accessories to go with it. As she got more confidence just by trying that dress on, we went to other dresses and she also tried on and bought another dress in white with a bold flowery print. She wore the polka dot dress to her son's wedding and phoned me afterwards to tell me that she felt wonderful in it and everyone complimented how beautiful she looked at the wedding. It was a great hit! She stepped out of her comfort zone and although I have lost touch with her through the years, I am sure she is enjoying a new affair with fashion and clothing as she becomes more visible in the world.

Now the question becomes somewhat of a paradox. "Are you afraid to let your true nature shine through by avoiding being seen, by not caring about your appearance because of fear; or are you hiding behind who you are by overdoing and overemphasizing how you dress and look to mask and overcompensate for your vulnerabilities?" The purpose of this work of mine is to help us find the appropriate balance for each one of us in the way we decorate our wonderful bodies to celebrate and communicate the truth of who we are and in that truth we actually make our contribution to world peace.

Tip: If you fall into the category of someone who is afraid to be seen (like the woman who was comfortable only wearing beige) I suggest that you invest in a journal and outline the older outfits you currently wear and mark how you feel when you wear them.

You are then ready to dip your big toe into the water so to speak and begin to take a few risks with your clothing by first investing in a few pieces of pastel tops to pair with your neutral bottoms. Then gradually add a few small prints in the pastels and some small pieces of jewelry – necklaces, earrings, and bracelets or watches. And as you begin to wear some of your new colors, journal how they made you feel as well as if anyone noticed them or complimented you on how you looked in them. Journal your feelings, such as fears, energy, challenges, joys, successes, feeling pretty or not, etc.

Take an inventory of your clothing and accessories and then make a wish list for filling in the gaps. I have included a form at the end of this to help you get started with your inventory.

## *My own experience of each color, style, line and texture and how I relate to them in my expression:*

I remember when I was graduating from college I wanted to move to Boston. My parents couldn't understand why I wanted to leave home. I told them "I need to find myself"...little did I know that I would be on the journey to finding myself, like in the 2010 Alice in Wonderland movie when the caterpillar asked her "Who are you?" for most of my life. Who would have thought that I would uncover who Diane is through the medium of fashion of clothing and colors? My teacher, Keshav, often has said, "You are the one being yearned for". I often wondered just who was yearning for me and realize now that it is simply Diane yearning to know Diane (spirit essence). There is no other person or being yearning for Diane – it is all Diane just like your entire world is all you and your divine essence is you as well. All of our searching for happiness and love is simply a longing for who we truly are!!! If I put it another say, it goes something like this: you are longing for spirit while at the same time spirit is longing for you. We are seeking for what and who we already are. Why? Because you and spirit are one and the same and we often search for things we think we have lost when they have been here right in front of us all the time. It is like looking for your eyeglasses when you had them on all the time!

Somewhere along the line through our conditioning, or rather our so-called socialization, we lost touch with our spirit. We separated ourselves from our true essence by identifying with an "idea" or "image" of who we think we are, forgetting who we really are. Who are you? It seems to me that we are in search of our own divinity...often times cloaked in our search for God or for our mate or the right career. We are searching for something that we already are, again, much like looking for your eyeglasses everywhere when you actually have them on your head. You can use clothing and color to help you discover this. You can gain access to your inner essence and learn how to communicate it outwardly and still fit in with the world while maintaining the integrity of the truth of who you are. You may not be able to find the words to describe who you are, however you can realize in a sense of a "knowing" that cannot be put into words about just who you are. Although I may not be able to tell you who I am except to introduce myself as a being named "Diane", I do know what I am not. I am not a body or an idea or concept that should or should not be or do this or that. I am Neti Neti (not this and not that) I simply "AM". "I AM". And I express that I AM in the various roles I play in this form. I must admit that there are times when I am not fully awake and I am grateful to have those moments of anxiety, fear, anger, guilt to point me back to remember who I am. They keep me humble. I am simply consciousness aware of itself. I have used my passion for fashion as the vehicle to remind me of who I am. I use it as healing tools that I can call upon in a moment's notice.

I have found that it is important to know my own inner sense of being when I awaken in the morning so I can communicate that sense or heal and soothe what may be ailing me or wasting energy either physically or spiritually upon rising. Decide what will bring you to feeling joy – it could simply be a favorite piece of jewelry, or sweater, or dress or even simply wearing something in your favorite color. Be tuned into what your state of being is, not necessarily to resist it, but to be aware of it, acknowledge it, embrace it, and treat it if you are so inclined ...

If you are doubting the existence of spirit in your everyday dress, just think back to a time when on Monday evening, for example, you decided to wear "x" to work on Tuesday, yet when you got up on Tuesday and attempted to wear "x" you either just couldn't put it on, or once you got it on, you had to take it off and wear something else. You can consciously employ spirit on a daily basis to guide what it needs to nurture it daily. Simply relaxing and taking a moment to allow it to guide you and being aware of who you are and what you are feeling on any particular day can be an invaluable tool to feeding your body, mind and spirit to meet and greet the day. It is a conscious effort. I call it "consciousness dressing".

It does help to know your own feelings about each of the colors of the rainbow, so I have designed a couple of Shamanic Journeys to assist you in determining how each of the colors overall makes you feel. They are included a bit later in this work.

I am of the opinion that what we wear is often a reflection of what we believe about ourselves, and this belief most often is not the truth of who we are. It often is a reflection of our mind's interpretation of the various symbols that we compare ourselves with based on what we have been exposed to through the media, our peers, our parents, bosses and our teachers. I spent the first 50 odd years of my life wishing I could be more like so and so. This changed with whomever I happened to admire in the moment. It could have been a colleague, a movie star, a singer, or some other person to idolize. It was anyone else but it was never me. This is a common illness of the entire human race. I don't think a bird wonders what it would be like to be a fish, and I don't think a fish wonders what it would be like to be an elephant. Our only true obligation as I see it, is to be completely ourselves while in form on the Earth.

Do you need to feel more feminine or masculine? What lies ahead of you for the day and what clothing will help you be more confident in communicating whatever needs to be presented that day? Are you dressing because you want to manipulate a situation or are you dressing because you want to express where you are at on any given day – or maybe you don't want to express it...It's really about knowing how to be comfortable in the world with who you are. Be aware that you are just playing a role in the world and if you view life as a play that you often play various roles and wear a costume that is fitting for that role, you can simply still be yourself in that role. Life is a cosmic play and we are all playing roles in the theater of life...and each of us has many different roles to play: worker, mom, daughter, sister, brother, friend, socializing, sexual being, wife, husband, personal trainer, carpenter, engineer, custodian, dancer, student, teacher, image consultant, Shaman, and on and on and on. Regardless of what role we are playing, we are divine beings in human form having a human experience.

Do you realize that American women are just as much a prisoner in their clothing as Middle Eastern women whose religion dictates what they can and cannot wear when we buy into the so called "rules" of fashion and dressing? i.e., can't wear white after Labor Day, only shiny glitz in the evening or at holiday time, must wear stockings, bras, girdles, short hair, long hair, high heels, kitten heels, boots, loafers, need to have a sexy body, need to look sexy....Why do you make yourself a prisoner with regard to what you wear? What fears lie underneath? What about the real you that you may be hiding? Who are you? My particular pathology of never feeling good enough or worthy enough is worth repeating here. We all have these fears and feelings of unworthiness at times and it is my hope to help you recoup your love of yourself and your divinity using the tools in this work as stepping-stones to that love.

Remember, I always wanted to wear what models and mannequins wore, so I gave myself permission to wear high fashion glamorous clothing – I loved them, the beauty and art in them, and I wanted to express my divine self, yet there was always the little Diane trying to also FIT IN with everyone, which seemed to necessitate looking like them – so at times I bought into that at the expense of being who I am or rather expressing my true self. Even though I knew I wasn't pretty enough to be a model I still wanted to feel like one. Of course, with the entire media blitz I didn't even know who I was. I had no idea that underneath the mask of the image of Diane was the essence of Diane...**a spiritual/ divine being who just happens to be in a human form so that spirit can experience, express and see itself as life in form**. I encourage you to unveil your true essence- your divinity. What is interesting about discovering my divinity has been the falling away of any feelings of lack as well as the falling away of any feelings of being better than anyone else, and there was and is a continuing of the falling away of comparing myself physically emotionally or spiritually to anyone or anything else. There is simply a feeling of EGO emptiness that is now filled with love and compassion. And there is no one at home taking credit for it. I have communicated this feeling by using the saying "The lights are on and nobody is home". That nobody I am referring to is the ego's image of Diane. By the way, divinity/essence has no gender just a tendency to project energy in an inner or outer manner depending on our spirit. To find out your true essence requires some exploration, both in determining what you are attracted to in relative reality as well as discovering your true essence in absolute reality.

I have developed a program designed to 'almost' take you step by step (actually, not in any particular order) on a journey to the beginning of discovering the truth of who you are and to blueprint an ideal wardrobe to assist you in communicating that truth... one that is as flexible as you are at any given moment in time. I say 'almost' because spirit is free and what I am working with are guides – not rules. We all have enough rules in our lives as it is. Where you go from here is entirely up to you. Are you ready to take the plunge into the depths of your true essence? There are NO RULES IN THIS PROGRAM. There are simply choices to make – some are based on survey facts and others will be based on your own feelings. Ideally, you will choose the third option, which is to open to spirit help you choose not only what you are going to wear on any given day, but also how you will live your life.

Did you know that everything in the universe is simply energy, and colors vibrate to different frequencies of energy and our attraction to colors impacts each of us in a different way? Your job is simply to explore and boldly go deeper into who you are than you have every dared to go before. (Are you seeing the Star Trek analogy?)

It's interesting that my studies in Shamanism and the work I have been doing on this program has made me question most of the learning I had studied in the area of clothing, colors and fashion – not because the studies weren't accurate based on thought and various studies, but rather because they failed to take into account the presence of spirit. Spirit, in my experience cannot be conceptualized or described in words. It can only be directly experienced. For me, using the tools of clothing and colors along with my studies in Shamanism has helped me tremendously in discovering and realizing the true spirit/essence of Diane. ***What I discovered along the way was the missing link in the world of fashion: the failure to truly link spirit with form.*** In order to do this, it is imperative that we discover who we are at our core essence. It is only then that we can more accurately apply the "yang" (form) of fashion to work in tandem with the "yin" (spirit); Yin should be leading Yang rather than Yang dictating to or leading Yin.

The following is taken from the Home Page of my website: www.clothesencounters.org:

"Who Are You?" Asked the wise blue caterpillar, Absolum, to Alice in the 2010 Disney movie "Alice in Wonderland" when he first encountered her. As the meeting progressed and he was asked by the other characters if she was the 'real' Alice, Absolum responded "not hardly". Is the image you are projecting to the world in your clothing and colors a true reflection of who you are? Is your image the real you or "hardly" you? Or, have you fallen victim to the dictates of fashion trends that tell you what styles and colors you should be wearing? When Alice's mother notices that she is not properly dressed Alice says "Who is to say what is proper? What if it was agreed that proper was wearing a codfish on your head, would you wear it?"[2] Are you wearing a 'codfish' just because it is the "in" thing to do, at the expense of the loss of who you truly are? At Clothes Encounters we will guide you on a journey using Shamanic journeying, creative art principles, eastern

---

[2]    Walt Disney, "Alice in Wonderland" Movie 2010

philosophy and mythology to a rediscovery of who you are at your core essence in order to help you create the image that reflects the truth of who you really are using clothing and colors. Reflecting your true image will foster increased self confidence, improve communication, and increase harmony and balance in your every day existence.

Take a ride down the rabbit hole with Clothes Encounters to explore, discover and uncover the hidden treasure of your true image. Learn how to let your image reflect the truth of you are at your core essence. Together we will peel away the layers of the false images you project out to the world based on your conditioning. Put and end to being a slave to the fashion police and FREE yourself from the prison of false images that comply with the status quo."

You can begin by asking yourself this important question: "Am I trying to win approval of my boss, friends, relatives, etc. by dressing in a way that will please him/her, much like the characters in the red queen's court in Alice in Wonderland did with faking defects in their physical form to win the queen's affection and approval?".....If you can answer "yes" to this in any way or form this program is definitely for you. Even if you answer "no" this program is still for you, if only because you are curious and like to have fun!

Like Alice, my own literal tumble down the rabbit hole occurred on March 9, 2013 while attending a Mitote held by my teacher Keshav Howe. We were split up into two groups during a 12 hour evening vigil intensive that began at 8:00 pm and ended at 8:00 am. Half of the group sat around an altar chanting various Hindu chants for an hour while the other half of the group went into another room to nap/sleep for an hour. Then, after the hour, the groups switched places. I was in the first group to sit around the altar and chant and while chanting I had the extreme sensation of spinning and turning and tumbling down a deep hole – the rabbit hole. I lost all sense of consciousness and my body – when I tried to get up to go to the other room to nap my physical body became like a rubber band and I was full of fear – I couldn't get up and walk – I had no control of anything at all. Keshav encouraged me to simply not resist the falling and going deeper down the rabbit hole and to breathe and ride out the fear. I complied and little by little and although feeling like Gumby I gradually began to Fall Together! As I fell together more and more there was an emptiness inside of me that was replaced with a sense of peace and freedom. Something left me that had been shadowing me all of my life – You could say it was my own self-importance – the Image of Diane fell away and in its place was an amazing feeling of love, peace and bliss. No Fear! I had been struck down. The experience was remarkably a lot like what had happened on the 4th of July in 1985 – the difference being that I had a teacher with me to help support me thru the journey down the rabbit hole. It took me a few hours to recover and I did not need tranquilizers to get me through it. Metaphorically I had died – my EGO died – and another layer of the false images of Diane was melting like the wicked witch in the Wizard of Oz.

Since 3/9/13 life has taken on a new meaning. Dressing has now become an even more fun undertaking for me as I play with different colors, styles and accessories to express and enhance my playful spirit. I have found that the more I open to spirit the more life comes to me. I no longer feel the need to chase rainbows – I am the rainbow – and I finally have my own acceptance and approval of me, just as "I AM" now in this moment.

I spent a lifetime shape shifting into various roles with my clothing as an aid to helping me feel accepted and loved. It is a very powerful healing tool. I feel it is one that we do not realize or utilize to its true potential.

If you are inclined to go even deeper than what this program does into your true nature, use this program as a bridge and find a spiritual teacher who can guide and take you all the way.

# CHAPTER 9

# *Your Divine Essence*

This work has been developed to assist you in determining which of the following Gods or Goddesses your essence truly reflects. I chose the prototypes of the gods and goddesses in order to help you remind yourself to connect with your divinity. I have also assigned each of the 5 elements to a god or goddess. This is simply a fun concept to help you remember your divinity. Are you an Athena, (Wood/Air); a Zeus (Metal); a Demeter (Earth), a Poseidon, (Water), or a Venus/Aphrodite (Fire)? Please do not worry about the specific gender of the god or goddess- because gender has nothing to do with this program with the exception of the importance of the need to have both feminine and masculine energies in balance. Some of us innately have more masculine energy dominant while others have more dominant feminine energy and it has absolutely nothing to do with sexual orientation. This program has to do more with the essence of each of these gods and or goddesses and the true essence of you. I have developed a questionnaire as well as a few Guided Journeys to assist you in determining which is most like you. When answering the questions please take care to respond to each one honestly about how you operate in the world MOST of the time....we are talking about the most dominant way you view and respond to life's situations. Within each Archetype there are various themes, with a common thread, however, we all have aspects of all the others operating within us and we may be in touch with a different god/goddess at a different time. Keep in mind that your dominant element will always be the same throughout your lifetime in this form.

You may be wondering what I mean by the Five (5) elements that can be keys t unlocking the mystery of your divinity. Chinese and Tibetan philosophies are based on the premise that all of life occurs within the circle of nature and that things in this 5 elemental nature of life are connected and mutually dependent upon each other. There are five (5) organ networks that I will refer to as 'causative factor' and are associated with the 5 elements of water, wood/air, fire, earth, and metal that can be utilized in helping determine which color and causative factor are dominant in each one of us and knowing how the elements interact and are interdependent can also help in using color selection in our clothing as a way to balance out our energy on any given day. I have also combined the characteristics of these elements with the color medicine associated with the 7 Chakras. This is because there also is a color associated with each of the 5 elements. It may be difficult to determine which of the elements is most dominant in each of us without the assistance of someone who has trained in it, however, later on I will attempt to give some hints as to some of the questions that could lead you to see which one you may lean towards. (More on this later)

## Color – The most powerful of the clothing symbols:

In the meantime, one of the first steps in this program as mentioned earlier is for you to determine how you "FEEL" about each of the 7 colors of the rainbow, black, white, neutrals, and the various lines, fabrics and styles of clothing. This should not be a thought process, but rather a "feeling" process and the best way to access your true feelings about anything is to take a journey into what I call "non ordinary reality" where you are not focusing on thoughts but rather your pure feelings – not the feelings that someone else imposed on you, or what fashion magazines dictate as being the "in " color this season.

I took a journey on my own as an experiment and here's what I came up with at that moment:

Red: makes me feel clear and definite and energetic, with a sense of confidence in myself

Orange: makes me feel happy, playful, carefree and outgoing

Yellow: makes me feel warm, bright and cheerful and compassionate

Green: makes me feel cozy and at home and safe and secure

Blue-turquoise: makes me feel beautiful, present, calm, positive, open and flowing

Indigo/Blue: makes me feel mysterious and deeply profound

Violet/purple: makes me feel wise and connected and whole

Magenta: makes me feel alive and connected to all of life

White: makes me divine, light, airy, pure and open

Black: helps me stay in the flow of tasks that need to be accomplished and makes me feel confident

Gray: makes me feel sad at times and truthful as well

Brown: makes me feel casual and earthy

Remember that each of the rainbow colors is affiliated with one of the 7 chakras in the body. Red - root chakra located at the base of spine or tailbone, Orange-Sacral chakra located in pelvis area, Yellow-solar plexus located in the stomach area, Green - Heart chakra located in the heart area, Blue-throat chakra located in the throat area, Indigo blue-third eye chakra located in the brow area above the base of the nose, and Violet or white - Crown chakra located at the crown of the head. It is very likely that the chakra associated with the color your journey disclosed is the one that may need balancing on that day, so why not listen to that calling and wear that color for the day. Everything I have learned about the Chakras and the colors that are associated with them points to the relative masculine and feminine energies each of them represents. The lower Chakras, which I will call "Yang" or masculine - root, sacral and solar plexus, relate more to humanity's outer physical energies, are connected by the Heart Chakra (which is at center-neither yin nor yang), to the upper Chakras "Yin" or feminine - throat, third eye, and crown Chakras. As most of you know, the yin/yang symbol is a circle divided in half by a curved line with half black (yin) and half white (Yang) each with a dot of the opposite color in the widest point. This tells me that the dominant masculine energy also needs a bit of feminine energy and vice versa in order that balance be kept. Another interesting fact is that without both darkness and light we cannot see color. There is an experiment you can do with a prism and some black and white checked wheels on paper to prove this. Without the black and white checks the colors cannot be reflected through the prism.

Each of the rainbow colors can also be categorized as yin or yang (feminine or masculine) and its opposite on the color wheel (or its complementary color) would be the added dot in the symbol. I have added the color "magenta" because it is a color that falls between red and violet and is considered a color of the highest order. And it seems to me it is no accident that its complement is Green - the color that represents the heart Chakra. For me, magenta also seems to connect the rainbow and chakras in a unified circle. According to Theo Gimbel in his "The Colour Therapy Workbook", magenta has a therapeutic use of facilitating changes, freedom, letting go of old habits no longer applicable and assists with the final transition into spirit at the correct time. The relative intensity of a color (how bright or soft a color is) also generates energy-bright are more outer, masculine, while pastels are softer and more inner/feminine.

Later on in the program I will provide you with a journey to discover your own true feelings about colors and styles.

## Getting in touch with your emotions for the day: Ask yourself the following questions:

Am I feeling clear and flowing, fearful, passionate and joyful, heartless or cold and unengaged, very compassionate, absorbed in myself, full of awe and wonderment, isolated and lonely, angry, jealous, frustrated or hopeful, organized and clear/direct?

Some suggested color prescriptions that have helped my energy are:

If I am feeling fearful and worried about making a mistake, I might want to wear blue or orange. If I am feeling cold and heartless and unengaged in life I could wear yellow, red or magenta. If I am absorbed in myself or on the pity pot I wear violet or yellow. If I am feeling isolated and lonely I sometimes wear my favorite color or orange. If I am feeling angry or jealous I will wear blue and avoid wearing red. When I am feeling like I need to be left alone, wearing white helps. White reflects the sun away, while black absorbs it. However, if you must be with others sometimes a bright color like orange or red or one that you like may help you feel more outgoing.

There are no bad colors; there are only the meanings that we attach to them. If we can isolate those illusory meanings from the truth numerous opportunities arise in how we can dress to express our true essence.

The question worth repeating becomes one of are you afraid of being seen by not caring about your appearance or are you going overboard with your appearance in order to be noticed? Oftentimes this is an indication that we are feeling a "lack" in some area of our lives. For most of my life I can honestly say that I went overboard with my appearance in order to be noticed hoping to finally be loved and approved of. I have recently realized that it was my own inner critic that didn't approve of me and as long as I am trying to sustain an "image" of perfection that inner critic will never be satisfied. It keeps me in samsara – the Buddhist word for suffering. This is the hamster wheel of "desire" a dis-ease that is running rampant in America. Have you ever noticed how the acquisition of something desired brings joy only for a moment? Before you know it, you are right back looking for something else to make you feel better, worthy, or loved. What if what we desire the most is simply to know who we are? Is it to connect with God? The only way to connect with God, in my experience, has been in those moments when I have seen and felt the God within me, not a separate God, but a God that is everywhere including in me. What a sublime discovery. The only way I have been able to experience this has been in those times that Ego has stopped trying to control me, and behaves like a guest – knowing when to leave and when to stay out of the way. Find out just what you are hiding and learn how to allow the truth of your divinity to be revealed with how you dress. This is one of life's paradoxes in the fashion arena. We need to find the appropriate balance.

I was always told I had a pretty face and had problems with weight. Because I never felt that I was pretty enough or worthy enough to wear beautiful fashionable avant garde clothing I often didn't take many risks with my clothing. Yet I loved all of it. It wasn't until 1974 when I moved back to Connecticut from Boston that I began to lose weight and like my body. I began to also have more confidence in attracting men. I began wearing more sexy clothes because I wanted to show off my new body. I also began to have an interest in fashion retail and worked in a high fashion store known as "Ups and Downs", however, I seemed to only have confidence in myself when I was thin. I began using models and mannequins as my standard of reference and I compared myself to everyone and everything I came into contact with. I have to admit that sometimes I thought I was pretty, but not very often, and I almost never loved my body at whatever weight it was at. Even at my very thinnest weight when my mother thought I looked anorexic I thought I was fat. It all boils down to my always feeling that I was not good enough or worthy of love-big time "lack". It truly went deeper than just being thin and looking good, because as you can see, even when I am or was thin I still hated myself deep down. I just didn't feel worthy of love.

It seems that today we women are either starving ourselves or eating ourselves into morbid obesity. We are killing ourselves. I happen to feel that this is because we do not know our own true nature or essence and we do not know or accept and love ourselves just as we are. This is not to say that when we know we are overweight that we should not take any action to reduce our weight. It simply means that we need to take a look at ourselves and begin to take care of our bodies and that means acknowledge the weight that we are at, and decide to be more conscious of what we are eating and eat healthier. For me, I tend to overeat and gain weight when I am emotionally upset, bored or confused. It seems that it is a compensation for a "lack" of some sort that I am feeling. Apparently on some level I do not feel that I am enough so I compensate for that by eating whenever I am frustrated or feeling upset. It is a hoarding of some sort I guess you might say. For me, I need to stop and ask myself each time I have a thought that I need to eat something, if I am truly hungry, or am I going to get something to eat out of boredom, loneliness, or feeling a lack or unworthy of love. In most cases my automatic reaction of going to the refrigerator or cabinet for a snack was and is either out of boredom, loneliness, or feeling unworthy. It has been a way of nurturing myself with the end result of actually punishing myself with feeling guilty and not to mention the sabotaging my weight loss or maintenance as the case may be-A Catch 22 I'd say! I noticed another interesting thing about me and my weight: It seems that my connection to gaining weight is that when I am heavy I do not attract men into my life and when I am thin I do. Somewhere underneath all of that is fear about being in an intimate relationship because I seem to have extra weight on me more often than not. This is something that I am working on even as I write this. The overweightness only adds to my feeling unworthy of love. It is a vicious cycle - a hamster wheel that I am slowly beginning to stop running on. I have now begun to really love my body and I am recognizing it as the temple that houses my spirit. As that temple, I am treating it with loving-kindness. I first show this loving kindness by what I decorate it with on the outside because this is something that I can see and feel an immediate response to in the form of beauty and feeling beautiful. When I am feeling beautiful I am totally connected to spirit. I am open and receptive to whatever life has to present to me. As I allow my spirit to love what I am wearing, it seems that it penetrates deeper into providing me with the feeling of worthiness. (It takes time to lose weight, but wearing clothes that make you feel beautiful and divine can have an immediate impact and it takes only a moment in time and perhaps a few extra dollars and you can feel and look fabulous in a few minutes!)

*I have also learned that all of life is a meditation...It all depends on what mantra you are telling yourself and I like to start my day with the mantra of looking and feeling beautiful.*

With this discovery I now get up each morning and ask myself what is going to make me "feel" good today, rather than what is going to make me look good. Ironically, I have found that what makes me feel good also makes me look good! That's what I call another "win/win". If I am uptight and anxious I ask myself: What color will help me be more open and flowing? It's like taking your temperature only it is more like a mood barometer. What is my mood du jour? Of course, there is a way to combine both of these energies and working with this program will help you integrate both of these important elements of your image, and to heal your spirit. I would like to point out that when I refer to "healing" I am not referring to "curing". It is my opinion that physicians have the power and credentials to "cure" our illnesses. I am not talking about "curing" illness, but rather "healing" spirit. Healing brings to my mind the fact that the body actually heals itself and that the way we dress can have an impact on helping the body heal itself by way of healing the spirit. I have found that living life in flow with the Tao is one of the ways to help heal our spirits.

I have always had a fascination with the yin/yang symbol and knew it was connected in some way to Taoism, however I had no true understanding of the Tao until I became exposed to Taoism during my studies with Keshav and it has had a profound influence on me. ...I now can see how clothing helps me to be in the flow of life like Taoism teaches. Taoism is often connected with the yin/yang symbol – signifying the importance of being in flow with change and maintaining a balance with nature, life, and the world. It is also interesting to note that the Star of David (a Jewish symbol) is in fact a representation of masculine (the top pointed pyramid) and feminine (the bottom pointed pyramid or chalice).

Recently I realized that I had lost my "much-ness" (Alice in Wonderland term from the 2010 movie) thru the years by blindly conforming to fashion trends and all the rules of society. I had always been referred to as a "free spirit" and somehow I lost much of it – my "much-ness" as the Mad Hatter would say. However, in fairness to myself and to my life as it has unfolded, I realize that every single thing, event, belief, etc. has lead me to who I am today. So I am not complaining. And while I cannot tell you in words who I am today, I feel that I am now able to express that in the clothing that I wear. I can also say who and what I am not. The journey for me has been an experience of weaving a cocoon of clothing around me for the various stages of my life as it unfolded. Sometimes feeling confident, and other times to make me feel more confident. Sometimes feeling loved and other times feeling the need to attract love. You get the picture. Now, I realize that what I am now wearing expresses who I truly am and how I feel on any day. The butterfly has emerged from the cocoon - no longer concerned with whether or not I am approved of, or looking beautiful, but rather what makes me 'feel' beautiful, free, loving and compassionate. What has actually happened is that the masks I was wearing to hide who I am have been shed to allow the essence of the 'who' I truly am shine forth. What masks are you wearing that are hiding your true divinity?

Like most women, In the past, I often complied with what I thought others would want me to wear out of fear of not fitting in - always needing approval. I spent most of my life living in fear of disapproval and also trying to be like someone else. While I am a proponent of having role models and mentors, a line needs to be drawn so as to not try to be just like that other person. We need to simply be our own best self. I spent a lot of time trying to be like someone else, and for a long time I lost sight of who I am.

Again, most of my life I spent comparing myself to models and mannequins and other women I met along the way. Who's fatter, skinnier, prettier, dresses better, attracts men, etc. You name it I compared it. I have learned that this is all mind, or EGO, seeking to take over the freedom I experience when embracing spirit and the truth of my divinity. We all have been conditioned. I have learned that jealousy is the killer of spirit, yet when I go deeper and open to jealousy I am able to open to and see the fear that is underneath it and then ultimately the love, compassion and vulnerability that it is afraid to expose.

In the pages that follow I refer again to the archetypes of a few gods and/or goddesses that each of us has a tendency to be similar to as it relates to our clothing style tendencies. This is not to pigeonhole you into a stereotype, but rather to be used as a pointer to the divine within you. What better way to feel your divinity than to be able to relate yourself to a god or goddess? It is also important to know that at times you will need to be in touch with the other gods/goddesses energy in order to assist you with your life experiences. The dominant divine archetype is not to pigeon hole you into another label, rather it is to give you a "knowing of your tendencies" similar to being right hand dominant, but that doesn't mean you don't do anything with your left hand. In fact, stepping out of your comfort zone is exactly what you will need to do to ignite your creativity!

Wearing structured suits keeps us more structured and focused however, we tend to be less creative when feeling confined. It keeps us in the realm of the known rather than accessing the unknown where true creativity lives. I recently brought a few suits to a consignment shop and they wouldn't take them in because suits are NOT selling at all. While I am disappointed that I won't be making any money on the sale of my suits, I am happy that we women are beginning to reclaim our femininity by no longer buying into the formal male corporate image that has dominated our culture and created separation for so long.

Are you afraid to even look inside and see that you are divine, that you are God, or are you fearful based on your religious background (which I might add is in my opinion just another control factor) calling you blasphemous and keeps you more encrusted in fear rather than in love?

My earliest recollection (something else worth repeating) of my connection to spirit and fashion was back when in 3rd or 4th grade in a Catholic grammar school and being fascinated by the nuns' habits. I loved the big sleeves and the rosary beads they wore around their waist, and even the head -gear. I also loved Jesus and wanted to marry him. When I went home to tell my mother I wanted to be a nun, she asked me why, and I told her because I liked their outfits. Her response was that that is vanity and nuns give up vanity and that is not the reason to become a nun. I also didn't want to give up men either. So I never became a nun; in fact I didn't even stay in that school much longer. Isn't it funny how the universe redirects us when we are in need of a redirection!

# CHAPTER 10

# *Practical magic: creating order out of chaos in your life using clothing and colors*

**FACT:** we don't have a lot of control over many things in general, but one thing we do have control over is the clothing we wear and how we organize our lives in our home. One way to begin to bring some semblance of order into our lives could be in organizing our wardrobes and our closets. The first steps in this process are to learn how you feel about clothing and colors and then to learn about the way you can use them to create more order and harmony in your life.

Before using the colors as listed below to assist you with your emotions and feelings, you will need to clear up any negative opinions and beliefs that you have about specific colors. So please do the following exercise in case you missed it previously.

## *COLORS*:

Using a Color Wheel determine how you feel about each of the rainbow colors. Include White, Black, Gray, and Brown. Write down your responses here:

Red
Orange
Yellow
Green

Blue (turquoise/cobalt)
Indigo (navy)
Violet (purple)
White
Black
Brown
Gray

Working with clothing and colors as spiritual healing tools occurs on different levels at different times in your life. I have explored them intensely in my life as well as in my business and feel it necessary to tell you that you will need to work with it at your own pace. Use some of the guidelines in this work as a starting point. There truly isn't any necessary order of things to do – it is whatever your spirit is inclined to work with at any moment in time. Do not rush yourselves – this could take many years or it could take a day, week, or month. Open yourself up to allow it to flow into you rather than going after it.

*I generally utilize the universal messages regarding Yin and Yang of the clothing & colors to communicate outwardly the messages I want to communicate and I use the Healing Model that follows later on in the program when I want to heal my own energy. It's not always possible to heal inwardly with the colors we want to communicate outwardly and for this reason I recommend that you invest in undergarments in the five elemental colors of : red, yellow, white, blue and green. It's a great way to handle both issues when in conflict with one stone.*

Some of my personal experiences with clothing and colors are as follows: To feel more passion and joy, or to feel more connected and wanting to connect more with others I wear red or orange; to feel more clear and flowing or to feel less overwhelmed I will wear blue or black; when I am "over doing" and I need to step back, I will wear white – I will also wear white to feel more awe and wonder or to simply want to be left alone and allowed to simply "be"; to feel more hopeful, organized, clear and direct I wear green or when angry; and to feel more nurturing and sympathetic/compassion for myself and others I will wear yellow. You can combine these color energies that are based on the elements with the colors that are associated with the 7 Chakras. They carry similar meanings as the colors associated with the elements. For example: green, while associated with the heart chakra, is also the color associated with the wood/air element and one might think that this is where compassion would resonate, which would be coming from having an open heart. You will note that green is a combination of a yin color (blue) and a yang color (yellow) and generally green is neither masculine nor feminine. It embraces both yin and yang in perfect balance, in my opinion. It is commonly associated with security. Blue, while associated with the throat chakra, and represents water with regard to the elements, helps one become more flowing and peaceful which is what truth and true communication are and our speech is spoken from the throat. Red is associated with the fire element and the base of the spine chakra and invokes passion and fire. Fire spreads rapidly and is full of energy which when worn can help one be more assertive as well as feel more physical energy and more grounded. Yellow, which is associated with the element of Earth and the Solar Plexus is the seat of compassion and nurturing. Often when feeling self critical or of others I will wear yellow to get in touch with true compassion. I will also wear yellow or its complement violet when my stomach is upset. Orange, which is a mixture of red and yellow is located in the sacral chakra and reproductive system. Interestingly it combines the colors associated with elements of fire and earth, the homes to compassion and passion. I like to wear orange when I want to be playful to attract fun and to not take things so seriously. It seems to connect my inner playfulness and lightness and friendliness with others. Purple and violet are associated with the Crown Chakra that is often referred to as the Chakra that connects us to spirit. I see it as a color combination of red and blue - and for me these two colors together represent balance and wholeness, which is in my opinion the essence of spirit and permeates everything. I like to wear purple/violet periodically to simply remind me that I am a spiritual being having a human experience. It reconnects me to my divinity on a moment's notice when I find that I am too deep in thought.

I also like to utilize the symbolism and feelings that I experience of line and style of clothing when deciding what I am going to wear on any given day. I often will either combine or substitute the energy of a particular line for a color to assist with my connection to spirit. So, it's important for your wardrobe to have a variety of line and styles as well as colors. I have a clothing capsule that combines this nicely and I use it when I am making presentations on Accessories Magic and The Closet Boutique. It also comes in handy for weekend getaways that fit into a single carry on bag. The capsule I speak about here is for spring and summer. Ideally, you should have one for fall and winter as well. Note that the dominant colors are yellow and red in my capsule and they both happen to be masculine and yang. Ideally, your capsule could be made up of one color in the yin family and the other in the yang family. However, many of my pieces are unstructured and flowing, which are from a more feminine yin family. Therefore, this capsule is balanced. So you see, there really is more than one way to the work with using your existing wardrobe to create balance in your inner and outer feelings and messages respectively. Note: the actual physical container of the clothing often serves as representing the masculine because it is made up of a form substance, while the color serves as the feminine aspect of the outfit. However going deeper into this you can look at the structure and line of the form as being masculine or feminine; as well as looking at the actual color as being either masculine or feminine. The items and explanations for my personal clothing capsule are as follows:

**Print top and bottom** - soft lines, unstructured. Note: my print has all the colors of the rainbow in it, so I can continue to build on my original capsule by simply adding the appropriate pieces in the other colors that are contained in the print. This is an exciting and easy way to build your wardrobe.

Red jacket and Red Slacks - hard lines, structured more formal masculine message

Red tank top – fitted-masculine

Yellow gauze top, jacket, and skirt - soft lines, unstructured, more feminine, pastel flowing message, yet yellow is a masculine color.

When I combine the red structured jacket with the yellow gauze unstructured skirt the combined energy emitted is a nice balance of both feminine and masculine energy that is also a combination of formal and informal. When I wear the Red Jacket and Pants as a structured suit the energy emitted is mostly masculine and more professional and more formal.

Note: you will need accessories in the two colors as well in order to coordinate the different looks so that there is balance and a nice flow to the looks while combining the two colors. I have a necklace, earrings and belt or bracelet in the red, and a necklace, earrings, and belt or bracelet in the yellow. I also like to have both silver and gold metal collars to hang pendants off of so that I can simply purchase various pendants with loop findings to mix and match. This saves money on jewelry since you are only paying for the pendants and not the cost of beads or the labor of stringing of beads on other pieces.

Tip: For those of you who do not have waist lines that are conducive to wearing belts, I suggest you use the third color in a bracelet rather than a belt.

Refer to the table that outlines the various outfits this capsule manifests for further details on working with the capsule.

Tip: You can build on your capsule with adding pieces in the other colors that are in your printed pieces, so I recommend you try and find a printed two piece set with multiple colors in order to give you the opportunity to expand your wardrobe each season and to update as various new styles are introduced by the fashion industry.

This Clothing Capsule Concept is also the perfect way to build a wardrobe from scratch!

# CLOTHING CAPSULE CONCEPT
# BASIC INVENTORY

| | CLOTHING | | | | ACCESSORIES | |
| | BEGIN WITH | | ADD LATER | | BEGIN WITH | ADD LATER |
|---|---|---|---|---|---|---|
| Color #1 | Jacket solid) | Bottom (solid) | Top (solid) | | 36" Beads Earrings | Pin Sash or Belt |
| Color #2 | Top (solid) | | Jacket (solid) | Bottom (solid) | 36" Beads Earrings | Pin Sash or Belt |
| Print with both Colors #1 & #2 | Top (print) | Bottom (print) | | | | |
| Miscellaneous | | | | | | 36"Beads in Silver or Gold Metal Earring Jackets s/g Metal Neck Collar Scarf in both colors |

The fabric that you choose for your capsule will depend on the season, your inner essence, your lifestyle, your budget and your career. Some of you are more casually oriented in your work while others are more formal. If you lean towards being more casual, earthy and athletic you might select fabrics that are rougher in texture. If you lean towards being more formal or conservative you might select fabrics that are smooth in texture. If you are more concerned with comfort and flowing in your clothing you might choose more natural fibers that are loose fitting. If you are one who likes to always be in style with what the fashion industry is prescribing you will more than likely have several capsules representing the entire gamut of style. Hopefully you have a budget that can support that!!! (Note: there are numerous discount department stores you can shop at that will be able to fulfill your 3 C's needs on your own budget.) When you get in touch with your true core essence, you will be better able to pare down your wardrobe and have more room in your closets. *Be sure to have items that are both structured and loose so that you can mix and match the masculine and feminine energies that are discussed in this work.*

# HOW TO PUT THE OUTFITS TOGETHER MATRIX

| OUTFIT #1 | OUTFIT #2 | OUTFIT #3 | OUTFIT #4 | OUTFIT #5 | OUTFIT #6 | OUTFIT #7 | OUTFIT #8 | OUTFIT #9 |
|---|---|---|---|---|---|---|---|---|
| C 1 | Print top | Print top | C 2 top | C 2 top | C 2 top | Print top | Print top | Print top |
| jacket | Print | C 1 | C 1 | C 2 | Print | C 2 | Print | Print |
| C 1 | bottom | jacket | bottom | bottom | bottom | bottom | bottom | bottom |
| bottom | C 1 | C 1 | C 1 | C 1 | C 1 | C 2 | C 1 | C 2 |
| C 2 top | jacket | bottom | bead/pin | bead/pin | bead/pin | bead/pin | bead/pin | bead/pin |
| C 2 | C 1 | C 2 | C 1 | C 1 | C 1 | C 2 | C 1 | C 2 |
| bead/pin | bead/pin | bead/pin | earrings | earrings | earrings | earrings | earrings | earrings |
| C 2 | C 1 | C 2 | C 1 belt | C 1 belt | C 1 belt | C 2 belt | C 1 belt | C 2 belt |
| earrings | earrings | earrings | | | | | | |
| C 2 belt | C 1 belt | C 2 belt | | | | | | |

# C=Color

The actual process that we are using in putting these outfits together is very simple. I call this process "ACCESSORIES MAGIC"!

1.  When putting two different colors together on the top and bottom, simply bring the bottom color to the top with your necklace and earrings.
2.  When wearing the same color top and bottom accessorize with your necklace, earrings, and belt (or bracelet) in a different color from your clothing, only keep the 3 accessory pieces in the same color. NOTE: YOU CAN CREATE NUMEROUS OUTFITS OUT OF A SIMPLE BLACK DRESS USING THIS TECHNIQUE!
3.  When putting on a jacket over a top of a different color, put a pin in the color of the top on the lapel of the jacket and add earrings in the same color.
4.  When wearing metals it is fine to only accent in two places when working with a solid dress, or same color top and bottom.
5.  If your figure is such that you do not feel comfortable wearing belts, you can use your 3rd place to accent with a bracelet.
6.  You can also add another look by using a print or solid scarf instead of a necklace.

NOTE: A few basic pieces of clothing you should always have on hand in addition to your two-color capsule colors are as follows:

black pants, brown pants, white pants, beige pants black top, white top, ivory top

black shoes, brown shoes, white shoes, beige shoes

black purse, brown purse, white purse, beige purse

pearl necklace and earrings

silver and gold tone collars

# BEFORE DECIDING ON YOUR CAPSULE COLORS IT IS ADVISABLE TO TAKE AN INVENTORY OF WHAT YOU ALREADY HAVE SO THAT YOU CAN BUILD ON YOUR EXISTING WARDROBE AND SAVE MONEY.

Wardrobe Design
INVENTORY

Only include those clothing pieces that fit you now. Discard anything that does not fit anymore whether or not it is too big or too small. We want to work with who you are now in this moment. Make an outline for each season of clothing, and if possible, sort by every day business, play, as well as colors, fabric texture, line, and style. Indicate which are your favorite pieces or outfits.

## *CLOTHING & ACCESSORIES*

| *CLOTHING* | **DESCRIPTION** | | | | | | |
|---|---|---|---|---|---|---|---|
| Tops | | | | | | | |
| Pants | | | | | | | |
| Jackets | | | | | | | |

| | | | | | | | |
|---|---|---|---|---|---|---|---|
| Skirts | | | | | | | |
| Dresses | | | | | | | |
| ***ACCESSORIES*** | | | | | | | |
| Necklaces | | | | | | | |
| Earrings | | | | | | | |
| Belts | | | | | | | |
| Scarves | | | | | | | |
| Shoes | | | | | | | |
| Purses | | | | | | | |

# MAP OUT YOUR OUTFITS HERE

Using the guidelines provided in the section regarding the Clothing Capsule Concept map out your outfits here. Be sure to include your currently very favorite outfits. You might like to journal your feelings about these favorite outfits with regard to how the texture, color and structure of each piece make you feel to give you some insight into what is going to make you feel special.

(Make copies of this chart as needed)

| NAME OF OUTFIT | TOP | BOTTOM | JACKET | ACCESSORIES |
|---|---|---|---|---|
|  |  |  |  |  |
|  |  |  |  |  |
|  |  |  |  |  |
|  |  |  |  |  |
|  |  |  |  |  |
|  |  |  |  |  |
|  |  |  |  |  |
|  |  |  |  |  |
|  |  |  |  |  |
|  |  |  |  |  |
|  |  |  |  |  |
|  |  |  |  |  |

Describe a few of your very favorite outfits. You can copy the chart above to list them out, and then comment on them on another piece of paper. What is the structure of each piece, what is the texture of the fabric, what is the dominant color, and write a few words about how you feel when you are wearing the outfit.

One of the key ways to begin this process of discovery of your divine true nature is to identify what masks you have been hiding behind. Your divine nature is and has always been with you, and it is your true nature that has simply been hidden behind a veil of illusions, and the process to accessing this divinity is to identify and drop the masks that you/we have so cleverly worn to protect it. Ironically, in the protecting of it, you are actually hurting yourself and pushing yourself away from your true self. It is a process of shedding masks rather than building masks. It is lifting the veil of illusion; a peeling away of the facade, so to speak.

Take some time to get to know your self a little bit better by answering the following questions in the following Life Styles Assessment. After each question ask yourself if it is true. You can use your responses to help you gain more knowledge about yourself and how you dress to express yourself.

# Life Style Assessment

## Your career/work!

What type of work do you do?

Are you more physical in your work like working with your hands (wait person, construction worker, yoga instructor, and physical trainer?

Does your work require you to wear a uniform? What color is it?

Do you work in an office? What is your job title? Is it a small office or a large office? Do people dress in suits or casual attire?

Is your work more about thinking and creating than manual "doing"?

Are you more inclined to be comfortable (and here I am not referring to physical comfort, rather I am referring to psychological comfort) in Jeans or loose fitting pants and/or skirts?

Does your work require you to be creative like in the arts?

Do you own your own business? What type of business is it?

Do you work in a factory doing assembly work?

Do you work in retail?

Are you a teacher or a Trainer?

Do you work in government? What branch or department?

Do you work with people or things?

What do you normally like to wear to work? Describe a typical workday outfit. Do you like wearing it? How does it make you feel?

In your work do you prefer to work independently, need support and direction, prefer to direct or lead others?

Do you like challenges in work or do you prefer routine repetitive tasks?

How do you feel about multitasking? How do you manage it?

## Your Social Life

What types of social activities do you participate in? Dancing at nightclubs, sports as a spectator, yoga, going to movies, going out to dinner in 5 star restaurants, or going out to dinner in regular chains like Friendlies, Panera Bread, TGIF's, Carraba's? Socializing with friends at your home or their home? Hosting parties and dinners? Playing cards and games? Going to casinos and gambling? Other- please be specific.

How do you dress for each of your social activities? Please list them out.

What % of your income would you say you spend on clothing and jewelry?

Are you more concerned with saving money than spending money? Do you need to feel financially secure?

Is it important to you to be wearing styles that are "in" and trendy?

Are you intimidated to wear something in a new look that doesn't fit into your comfort zone?

Is it important for you to wear accessories such as a scarf, jewelry, shoes that go with your outfit?

Do you prefer wearing slacks or skirts?

Do you like to wear high heels (whether or not your feet don't)?

How do you feel about being noticed and/or being the center of attention?

Do you like to feel good about how you look? Do you care about how you look?

Is it important for you to be impeccable with your appearance?

Are you afraid to draw attention to yourself?

Would you like to be more daring in your clothing and color choices? If so, why?

## **Personal grooming**

Is your hair long or short? What do you do daily to "do your hair"? Do you prefer a hairdo that doesn't require you to set your hair, blow dry it or curl iron it?

Do you color your hair? Are you comfortable with letting your hair color be natural or going gray?

If you color your hair why do you do it?

Have you ever had cosmetic surgery? If so, what have you done? Why did you do it? How did you feel about yourself afterwards? If you have not had cosmetic surgery would you like to have it? If so, what is holding you back?

Do you wear make up? How often: Daily or only on special occasions? How about at the gym, do you wear it at the gym?

Have you ever had a color analysis done? If so, what did you learn from it and was it helpful to you in selecting clothing?

## **How you feel about style**

Is there a style of clothing or a color that you would love to wear, but are afraid to wear it? If so, what is it? Why are you afraid to wear it? Do you know why?

What would you love to wear if you did not care what others thought of what you are wearing ? Why haven't you worn it? What fear, if any, is attached to it?

Is it because of your weight? or that you have no occasion to wear it?,

Do you enjoy shopping for clothing? What types of stores do you like to shop in for your clothing? Department stores, Discount Department stores, Boutiques, or do you prefer to buy clothes from catalogs or via the Internet?

Do you set trends or do you prefer to follow trends? Or, do you simply not care about trends at all?

What is your relationship with your body? Do you like what you see? Is it serving you well? Are you grateful for your body? Are you serving it well? How do you take care of it?

**Assignment:** go out and try on the outfit that you would love to wear and notice how it makes you feel to wear it. If the feelings are positive, and you can afford to buy it, buy it and find an occasion to wear it. If necessary, create an occasion. Take yourself out on a date where you could wear this. Go out to dinner alone - taking yourself out on a date. Make sure that you feel absolutely wonderful in this outfit. Look at yourself in the mirror both front and back. Style your hair like you would love to have it look and wear make up that makes you feel beautiful.

The above Life Style Assessment is not a test. It is simply a tool for you to use in helping you to spiral into the rabbit hole and work your way back up and out once you have worked on the discovery of your true divinity.

You may not have ever thought about it, but knowing your Elemental Color/Causative Factor (Note: We are all profoundly related to one element more than the other four) and the discovery of your true essence/divinity can actually help you see whether or not your chosen career path is in sync with your essence. This is not to say that you need to change your career, however it may actually give you some insight into why dissonance sometimes pops up in the working environment. My experience in working with clients has been that it revealed in them answers as to why they were feeling a need to change in their careers.

We touched upon the five (5) elements previously and her I will now go into my experiences with them.

# CHAPTER 11

# *The 5 Elements, The 7 Chakras & The God/Goddess Connection*

My research and studies into Chinese and Tibetan spiritual healing, Eastern philosophies regarding the 7 Chakras, studies with Master Shaman Keshav Howe and more importantly my direct experience, have brought about some interesting conclusions regarding how colors, clothing and characteristics of the 5 elements (wood/air, fire, earth, metal and water) and the 7 Chakras impact and can be utilized to promote spiritual healing. The following are my observations, conclusions, and recommendations for using the various colors in your selection of clothing to promote healing as it relates to each of the elemental causative factors for each particular element.

I will start with my own, and you will see that I have much more to say about my own experiences than about the others due to having explored myself more extensively throughout the years.

Most of the healing energies I am suggesting are based on Chinese and Tibetan philosophies regarding the 5 elements of wood/air, fire, earth, metal and water and how their energy flows within the human body. In general some of the information that follows came from my digestion and interpretations of the teachings of Master Shaman- Keshav Howe and some reading in the book: "Between Heaven and Earth – A Guide to Chinese Medicine" by Harriet Beinfield, L.Ac. and Efrem Korngold, L.Ac., O.M.D. Each of the 5 elements is represented by relationships between two or more causative factors as I refer to them, and their flow within the body. The element of Fire has 4 organs associated within it:

(Heart (yin), Small Intestine(yang), Heart Protector,(yin) and Triple Heater(yang). The element of Water has the 2 organs of Kidney(yin) and Bladder(yang) associated with it. The element of Wood/Air has the 2 organs of Liver(yin) and Gall Bladder(yang) associated with it. The element of Metal has the 2 organs of Lungs(yin) and Colon(yang) associated with it and the element of Earth has the 2 organs of Spleen(yin) and Stomach(yang) associated with it. Each element has a color associated with it as well and these colors will play an important role in the colors suggested in this program for you choose to wear to help heal and balance your spiritual energy. The colors are as follows: Fire/Red, Water/Blue, Wood/Air/Green, Metal/White, and Earth/Yellow. (More on the colors will be discussed later). Keep in mind that the color therapy I am suggesting is based entirely on my own interpretation and experience with these causative factors and the colors associated with them.

There is an order in which the energy (or Chi) of these organs flows in the body and it all starts with the Fire element's Heart. Heart (I) energy flows into Small Intestine (II), which flows into the Water element first into the Bladder (III), which flows into the Kidney (IV). Next, the Kidney (IV) flows back to the Fire element's Heart Protector (V) and then on to the Fire Triple Heater (VI). From the Fire Triple Heater the flow enters the Wood/Air element's Gall Bladder (VII), which then flows, into the Liver (VII) and from the Wood/Air element into the Metal element's Lungs (IX), which then flows into its Colon (X), and the Metal element flows into the Earth Element's Stomach (XI) on to its Spleen (XII). From the Earth's Spleen (XII) the cycle begins again with its flow into the Heart (I). You do not have to know or memorize these cycles to enjoy the benefits of the healing energies associated with the colors and each of the elements that I will discuss later on in the program. However, it is important that you learn which of the elements is your own dominant element (causative factor) that is a pointer to the areas that you often go in and out of balance and will be a key to knowing how to use color to help heal those energy imbalances. There are other relationships between the various elements which I will discuss a little bit further on because these relationships will help in dealing with the various positive and negative attributes and tendencies of each of the element's causative factors. I will now cover some of the basics about the causative factors before going into the healing model because the first step is to determine which of the causative factors is dominant in you.

The 5 elemental causative factors do have physical characteristics associated with each of them. These characteristics are: color around the eyes and mouth; natural body odor; and sound of voice. There are other attributes common to each of the elements such as emotional extremes when going in and out of balance. There is a grid at the end of this book that covers the other characteristics of the various 5 elements and their causative factors. Your elemental causative factor is with you for your entire life in this body. Healing your spirit from the point of your elemental causative factor can take many forms. Using clothing and color is a piece of the puzzle.

> Note: This program is based on my knowledge and experiences of the 5 causative factors of wood/air, fire, earth, metal, and water and the 7 Chakras. Most of the actual healing elements are in reference to the causative factors. I work with the colors of the Chakras and their location in the physical body as an enhancement. I tend to use the Chakra colors as tools to enhance my physical well-being and to communicate outwardly what I want to communicate to the world.

**A word of caution here: None of this is to be construed as medical advice – I am talking about healing on a spiritual level that can and often does impact our physical being. It should never be used instead of seeing a professional medical practitioner for any illness.**

I have also assigned each of the elements to a god and/or goddess archetype to assist the reader in identifying with their own divinity. This is not to make you a prisoner of your archetype because, as mentioned earlier, just like you may be right or left handed you often use the non-dominant hand to assist you in life. Even though the archetype will be with you for all of your life it is good to know the basics about the non-dominant archetypes as well so that you can use them when your energy level relative to their causative factor is deficient and you need their energy.

- Wood/Air (I liken to the goddess Athena-Goddess of Wisdom and Crafts, Strategist and Father's Daughter[3]

In my opinion the wood/air element is the most versatile of the 5 elemental causative factors as far as they relate style and dressing. Perhaps I am prejudiced about this because I am a Wood, however, what I am saying appears to ring true based on my experiences with myself as well as with others who also happen to be woods. The organ network associated with Wood/Air is the liver and gall bladder – the architect and contractor of life and the color associated with wood/air is green. Woods are very action oriented people (notice that our traffic light color "green" means "go") with a passion for "doing", hence they often are risk takers. Like Athena "...martial and domestic skills...involve planning and execution, activities that require purposeful thinking. Strategy,

---

[3]    Bolen, M.D., Jean Shinoda; "Goddesses in Everywoman, Page 76

practicality, and tangible results are hallmarks of her particular wisdom. Athena values rational thinking and stands for the domination of will and intellect over instinct and nature. Her spirit is found in the city; for Athena the wilderness is to be tamed and subdued.[4]

Wood's physical characteristics are: green around the eyes and mouth, emitting an odor like burnt butter or urine, and a shouting voice. Wood emotions often range from being hopeful, organized and direct to jealousy, anger and frustration. They have a passion "to do" and get their feelings of security from the completion of whatever needs to be done. They are creative, detailed oriented, organized, hopeful, visionary, coordinated and great planners. However, when out of balance they can be shortsighted, hopeless, rigid, jealous, inflexible, critical, judgmental, controlling and a perfectionist. That being said, in relationship, Woods in balance often are competent, present and involved; yet with the other side of the coin can also be impatient, competitive and manipulative. Woods, when in flow with their positive aspects, will be Pioneers in their dressing and often are the most creative with their wardrobes. They will strategically decide what to wear based on what needs to be accomplished during the day or evening in combination with how they are feeling inside. They are courageous in that they will try new things without worrying about what other people think. Because they are more daring in their approach to life they often have a lot of dramatic or romantic/dramatic pieces in their wardrobes. When they are out of balance or experiencing a "lack of wood" aspect, that is, when they are not in flow with regard to their causative factor, they may tend to be more casual in their dress in general and not pay attention to details. In balance Athena is a pioneer and a leader and doesn't worry about what

---

[4]     Bolen, M.D., Jean Shinoda; "Goddesses in Everywoman", Page 76

other people think about how she dresses. She is in touch with her energy daily and dresses accordingly.

Athena, in balance, is not afraid to be seen and often will take risks with her clothing as well as taking a very active role in life as leaders. Athena often dresses with a more creative approach to the latest styles. They will usually combine masculine clothing traits along with more feminine fashion trends and always will have something in their wardrobe of what's "in" and lean towards bright and clear colors regardless of their personal coloring. She often will wear a headdress or hat and accessories.

**Energy prescriptions**: As a wood, with the color Green associated with it, when I need to take some action I often will wear the color green. In fact when I sense unrest in my body or mind I will first connect with the color green – either think green or wear green underwear. This is so if I want to wear another color outwardly I still have the benefit of having connected with the action I need to take. If there is no unrest in my body or mind sensed at all I will wear whatever color seems to make me feel happy that day.

Because of their passion to do, Woods/Athena's have a tendency to over do and try too hard and sometimes will become overly aggressively trying to accomplish something or other: when this happens Athena's can get in touch with the energy of Metal, which has a relationship as the mother of Wood, and wear white, the color associated with Metal, to help be more still, silent, and to make things more simple. White helps me to let go of things and in that letting go I open up to what is present and I am better able to go with the flow. It is important too to get in touch with the causative factor (Wood) before employing any other prescription so I may think green or wear green eye shadow or green underwear to connect with my Wood as well.

Another trait of Wood can be tunnel vision and narrow mindedness. When this occurs I am not in flow with life and I will nurture myself with wearing the color blue. Blue is the color of Water and Water nurtures Wood. When my physical energy and passion for life is down (this can also be related to 'losing heart') I will wear red. I will also use Blue to help me when I am angry or resisting what is happening in life. I use yellow when I find that I am judging and needing to feel more compassion for myself as well as others. The element of Wood often restrains Earth (represented by the color yellow) and is considered the mother of Earth; and reconnecting with Earth/yellow acts like a vaccine for me when I am lacking compassion. I resonate towards white when I feel doubt and need to feel deserving of love and respect. Violet seems to help my intuition and creativity along with a bit of yellow. My metal of choice is silver – as I connect with the moon and with my hair, skin and eye coloring. Because water (blue) nourishes/engenders wood and metal (white) restrains wood, I like to use blues and whites to help me be more in flow with life (blue) and white to stop and relax when over active. When I am in perfect balance as a wood I am flexible like a willow tree and I simply wear any color I am drawn to in that moment.

I also often combine the energies of the colors with the energy of the particular line and fabric of the clothing to help me stay in flow with what I have ahead of me during the day as well as how I am feeling. This is where the true creativity comes in and the utilization of combining yin and yang of my outfit for the day. In this context I refer to the yin as how I am feeling and the yang as to what I need to communicate outwardly to the audience of the day. I have found that I need to be in sync with my own daily energy (yin) as well as the people and event(s) I am engaging in for the day (yang). Sometimes this means wearing colored underwear that doesn't show outwardly to help me with my own energy level that day that perhaps I do not want to communicate outwardly. Get the picture? Play with this. Remember that clothing is the container for the color and the line of clothing can either be yin or yang. So, if the situation calls for me to wear a yang color like red or hot pink, I might wear a soft flowing broomstick skirt as the yin! It's a lot of fun and it doesn't hurt anybody. I will wear soft textures and flowing lines to help me lighten up, and firmer textures with straight lines to help me be more focused. When I want to be more outgoing I often will say it with a print in warm vibrant color. When I am feeling impatient I will wear yellow for more compassion and blue to put me back in flow. The color White helps me to be still. When I become inert I will revert to green for my "get up and go".

Color isn't the only clothing symbol that can serve to heal our spirits. I often combine the other clothing symbols of line, texture, and details incorporating both the masculine and feminine energies (yin and yang) daily. For example: when wearing red, which is a masculine color, I often will either wear a soft fabric with an unstructured line (yin) to balance the impact of the color red. Most of my white (yang) clothing is soft unstructured fabric that brings in the yin of the outfit for balance. Please refer to the previous sections regarding the yin and yang of clothing and colors for information about the masculine and feminine energies of all the clothing symbols and work with them to address your energetic needs daily.

- Fire: (I liken to the goddesses Aphrodite and Venus-"Symbolize the transformative and creative power of love. Aphrodite (Venus) was an awesome presence who caused mortals and deities to fall in love and conceive new life."[5]

Fire's will often dress in a more dramatic and sexy way that expresses their passion and desire to be close. The organ

---

[5]    Bolen, M.D., Jean Shinoda; "Goddesses in Everywoman" 2004, Page 224

network associated with Fire is the heart /small intestine, the triple heater/heart protector and the color associated with Fire is Red. Physical characteristics of Fires are: the color red around the eyes and mouth, an odor like burnt ash, and tendency to often laugh inappropriately or have an inability to laugh. Fire's sometimes fall within the category of "lack of fire" and in this instance they may display a more whitish/ashen color around the eyes and are often mistaken as a Metal (more on Metal later). Some positive attributes of Aphrodite when she is in balance are her compassion, warmth, enthusiasm, sunny disposition and playfulness. She is often associated with sexuality. When out of balance she often displays sexual coldness, vulnerability, heartlessness and emotional coldness. I often associate Fire with Spirit like the burning bush that Moses encountered. We often say that things go up in smoke. I often let go of things that are bothering me by writing them down on a piece of paper and sacrificing them to my fire pit. Fires are the Wizards of the world in that they have the uncanny ability to unite human aspirations with divine purpose. Fires can use clothing and colors to improve their communication and to develop harmonious relationships. Ironically, they can appear to be unapproachable and/or unfriendly when they make the bold statements and dress too sexy. Red, the color of Fire, has gotten the label of making people see and feel aggressive. However, using the softer lines and patterns with the color Red can soften the message. Fires who are experiencing "lack of fire" may lean more towards conservative styles of an Earth (Demeter) or a Metal (Zeus). To perk themselves up they could wear red, orange or hot pink to assist in bringing out their spirit and to help with communication and relationships. When too fiery and overly aggressive, fires can cool down their wardrobes by wearing blues (the color of Water) and softer fabrics. Water is the Mother of Fire and can help to restrain fire when it becomes too hot or spreads too rapidly. Combining these colors and textures with the boldness of fire's tendency towards the dramatic can morph into becoming more approachable with not much effort and that alone can have a profound effect in increasing healthy communication. When experiencing or feeling needy Aphrodite can wear green (the color associated with Wood) to nurture herself and to stoke up the Fire. Wood nurtures fire.

**Energy Prescriptions**: Fires sometimes do not know how to discern what is good and because they sometimes do not let go of what should be eliminated, perhaps in the form of forgiveness, they often find themselves in unhealthy relationships. Fires can wear red to re-ignite their passion and kindle their hearts, yellow to have more compassion and violet to soften their drama. Fire is restrained by water (blue) and restrains metal (white) so when fire needs to simmer down they might want to wear blue and when needing to wash away anger, and white to help them let go of things that are eating away at them. In fact, using the combination of Blue and White can be quite healing for Fire. Fire is nourished by wood/air so wearing green can help reconnect them with their need to reestablish their direction and take action when they are lost to help them move on beyond the hurt. Wood feeds fire so when feeling cold and heartless fires could wear green, the color associated with wood. Fires when feeling over passionate can use blue to simmer down and turn down the flame. Fire nourishes Earth when it turns to ash thus contributing to Earth's Compassion. The color yellow is associated with Earth and Fire can also tap into Earth's Compassion by wearing yellow.

- Earth (I liken to the goddess Demeter-The mother archetype that "motivates people to nurture others to be generous and giving and to find satisfaction as caretakers and providers")[6]

Earths, when in balance, are generally grounded, understanding, balanced, stable and secured with an uncanny ability to fully digest life. They are the Peacemakers in the world. They have a gift of mediating and turning conflict into harmony. Earth's are like chameleons adapting themselves to the attributes of those around them developing an environment of trust. When out of balance they often display the negative attributes of excessive worrying, being needy, depressed, stingy, starved for attention or overindulgent. The organ network associated with Earth is the Stomach/Spleen and the color associated with Earth is yellow. They have an obsession "to have" and sometimes tend to overeat, and over indulge in collecting things. Their natural body odor tends to be sweet and fragrant and the voices tend to come across as singing. Earth's tend to dress more casually and in softer earth colors like yellows, soft oranges and browns. They are not very dramatic in their choice of clothing. They can also lean towards more feminine and smoother/softer lines and small prints in their choices of clothing and colors. They prefer small to medium sized dots, floral, paisleys, and lean more towards curved lines in their clothing. They have a softer approach to life rather than a structured approach. They lean towards more comfortable clothing with a casual feel and rougher textured fabrics or a look that connects them more to the Earth. They prefer unstructured and loose fitting clothing or sports clothes that show off an athletic figure. Earth's may often look too casual

---

[6]   Bolen, M.D., Jean Shinoda; "Goddesses in Everywoman", 2004, Page 172

for business or important events and should pay more attention to details in their dress if they want to attract people to their businesses and be taken more seriously.

**Energy Prescriptions**: Earths when out of balance can become very self-absorbed and can be full of profound sympathy that can lead them to being perceived as lazy. They also can be starved for attention, worry excessively, become needy, stingy and overindulgent. To help overcome these feelings and shake things up a bit Earths could wear red or orange to nurture their spirit because fire nurtures earth. Red can help to ignite passion, orange to help with depression and green to spur to action to stop and overcome excessive worrying. This is because Fire nourishes earth and wood restrains earth. When feeling overly sympathetic or self-absorbed Earths could wear green to spur them to action because Wood is the mother of earth. Earth nourishes metal. When feeling self absorbed, depressed, lazy and insecure Earths could wear green to help return to their normal optimistic cherishing and understanding. Earth should always wear some yellow in order to anchor themselves to their natural grounded, stable and balanced attributes. Wood restrains Earth and remember Wood is the Action element, which is why wearing green can help give Earth the jump start to action when feeling overly sympathetic and/or self absorbed.

- Metal: (I liken to the god Zeus-The god who appears as light and brings light and consciousness to the humans...[7])

Metals are the Alchemists in the world and are associated with the Father, hence Zeus in Mythology. They seek perfection as it relates to form and function. Metals are associated with Buddha

---

[7]    Bolen, M.D., Jean Shinoda; "Gods in Everyman", 1989, Page 45

Wisdom. Metals are often represented as the Father. Metals seek to purify life, which is why the color white represents metal. Snow is white and if you pay attention, when it blankets the earth it creates a pure and pristine look and feel to the environment. Notice during a winter snowfall how silent the earth is as the snow gently descends and blankets the earth. In the arena of clothing, metals tend to simply use it for function. Metals are the least likely element to be concerned with their appearance and basically look for pure and simple looks. The organic network associated with their element is the lung and the colon and the color associated with this element is White. Their positive attributes are purity, clarity, fatherly, self- respectful, and they have the ability to let go of things. Their negative attributes of being unyielding, brittle, stagnant, dismissive, isolated and lonely manifest when they are out of balance and unyielding. There are fewer Metals in the world than any of the other elements. They are very traditional, functional, and lean towards straight lines in style of dress. They use more solid colors than patterns, and smooth fabrics rather than rough fabrics. They dislike dressing for show. Often times they need to take some time to coordinate their looks for business and special events if they are interested in attracting relationships and business. In private they would wear whatever is most comfortable and functional.

**Energy Prescriptions:** Fire restrains metal by its ability to burn and melt metal; and when metals are feeling isolated and lonely they can wear red, or orange to help stimulate them and blue to stimulate communicating. This is because Fire is the mother of Metal and controls or restrains Metal. Metal is nourished and supported by Earth that helps permeate it with refined substances that enhance its life giving properties so wearing yellow can be used to lighten up and have more compassion. Metal restrains wood so when a Metal finds himself overdoing it he can wear white to slow down and green to get up and go. Because metals can be dull, rigid and non responsive in relationships they can use green (the color of wood) or red (the color of fire) to become more involved, competent and present. Metal has a nurturing relationship with water as it can purify water. Metal/Zeus is content to simply "be" and this element with the color "white" can help all of the other elements simply stop and become present in the Now, however it is absolutely necessary for Wood/Athena to remember the father – and simply let things go to get back into presence.

- Water: (I liken to the god Poseidon-"As god of the sea, Poseidon represents the unconscious. In its shallows just below the surface lies emotions and memories...the collective unconscious.")[8]

The element of Water resonates to the colors blue and black. Waters are often depicted as the Philosophers and explorers of the deep, like the god Poseidon. They are often in search for the truth and have a passion to know. Waters are natural explorers of the deep unknown. Blue is also the color associated with the throat Chakra and truth. The organ network that is associated with water is the kidney/bladder. Because Water flow alternates with periods of rest (ice in winter) and movement, it has the capacity to support active or outward clothing expressions and inward directed non-attention getting clothing. Waters' search for meaning transcends the day-to -day concerns of humanity. Waters left to their own devices are thinkers rather than doers and to that end tend to be conservative in their dress. They often play it safe with conservative styles that are of medium scale in size, and often

---

8    Bolen, M.D., Jean Shinoda; "Gods in Everyman", 1989, Page 73

well tailored.. There are no styles that waters need to avoid as long as everything is medium in scale and not exaggerated if they want to remain comfortable and at ease in their dress. This gives them similar flexibility in clothing choices as the Wood/Air element, however Waters will usually not be the first to try something new and usually are not daring in her clothing and color choices. They often do not dress to attract attention. Waters will tend to use fabrics that are smooth to medium in texture (tweeds), medium scale polka dots, paisley, floral and geometrics that may be slightly stylized but not too fussy. They wear medium stripes and plaids as well. Waters need to be careful that their wardrobe doesn't get too boring and could add some interesting accessories from the other personalities to perk up their looks. Waters often stay away from bright colors except to use as an accent. Waters also tend to lean towards clean monochromatic schemes.

**Energy Prescriptions:** Earth restrains water much like a dam, and when a person who is a Water Element is either too rigid or lacking boundaries the color yellow can be used to help temper the flow of water. Red can be used to melt the icy periods or perk up complacency. Violet will help stop thinking too much and opening up to allow spirit and intuition in. Metal nourishes water so white can also be used to help waters overcome fears. When in flow, Waters can choose any color to wear depending on what they are drawn to.

Color isn't the only clothing symbol that can serve to heal our spirits. I often combine the other clothing symbols' energies of line, texture, and details incorporating both the masculine and feminine energies (yin and yang) daily. For example: when wearing red a masculine color, I often will wear a soft fabric with an unstructured line (yin) to balance the impact (yang) of the color red. Most of my white (yang) clothing is soft unstructured fabric that brings in the yin of the outfit for balance. Please refer to the previous sections regarding the yin and yang of clothing and colors for information about the masculine and feminine energies of all the clothing symbols and work with them to address your energetic needs daily.

# CHAPTER 12

# *Additional observations and color techniques based on my own personal experiences*

It is very important not to overlook the effect of our dislikes of various colors and the role they can play in using the healing properties of color in our every day lives. I have found that when I do not like a particular color it helps to know what feelings it brings up and also to remember if there is a story that goes along with it that also needs to be healed, keeping in mind that it is the story that keeps us suffering. I often recommend that you begin to wear the color that you dislike in small doses in order to help you heal from the dislike of it, much like the antidote to a poison is found in the actual poison itself. Remember, there are no bad colors – just our attachments to the meanings we place on them. I like to use the universal messages of clothing and colors and the elemental colors to help me transcend the erroneous meanings that "mind" gives them that keep me suffering.

**Violet** – Since violet is a blending of both red and blue and red is the color associated with the element of fire and blue is the color associated with the element of water these two colors will have a dominant role in working with and balancing your energy level on any given day. Interestingly enough, red and blue are complements in the color wheel. As an Athena with a lot of Venus attributes myself, I have found that I am naturally attracted to reds, blues and violets in my selection of clothing. However, these colors represent my two extremes of passion and calmness and I use red to increase my passion and energy and blue to temper and calm myself when overly excited. Violet is the color that connects our Crown Chakra to spirit (or the divine), and when this connection is realized I am in total balance. I wear the color violet to help me feel that connection. However, in Chinese medicine I am a Wood/Air element with a passion for action and doing. As mentioned earlier, the color associated with the Wood/Air element is Green and Woods are often described as being the Pioneers in life. Although I am a Wood/Air element I also have the presence of a lot of the element of Fire in my being, so red and blue play a major role in impacting my energy level on any given day. Red because it represents fire and blue because it represents its opposite of water that so happens to be the element that "restrains" fire. The dominant organs in the body for a wood are the liver and the gall bladder (that represent the architect (planner) and the contractor of the body). When I think of the color green I often think of growth that happens to be an action oriented noun. As a Pioneer, Woods are often the first to experiment with new styles. Elemental woods have a passion "to do" (often referred to as Karma) and when in the doing mode I need to be focused so I will wear the color green to help me become more focused and disciplined to do the task at hand. Oddly enough, the color Green is also often times associated with security as is portrayed in the color of our money. It is a nurturing color that often times makes me feel safe. As a wood I often lack patience and compassion for myself as well as for others. Green is a nurturing color because it is a mixture of the colors blue and yellow, while at the same time being a complement to the colors red and magenta. When I am able to stop and notice that I am out of balance with my patience and compassion I sometimes will wear yellow to help me return. Yellow is the color of the element of Earth and is also associated with compassion.

**Red** –Red is associated with the Base Chakra, the one that connects us to the earth. It also represents the element of fire and fire is hot. When we are passionate about something we often say that we are "on fire" about it, be it in a romantic way or in a creative way. Red is drama and spurs me to action when I am feeling lethargic and bored. It ignites my passion. It is a color that can be seen clearly from afar and people who are not afraid to be seen often wear red. If you find yourself in dislike of the color red, take a look at how you feel about being noticed. Are you in hiding because you do not feel worthy of being seen? You might try gradually reconnecting with the color red by gradually wearing pinks and going into fuchsia/magenta as you begin to change the expression of your essence. Red in small doses such as a scarf or accenting with jewelry is also a good way to gradually exposing yourself to the color which will actually help you to use the color to heal you in those times when feeling the "blues"

Red is a primary color and is often associated with passion and fire and is considered a very dramatic color. I use red to help me get energized when feeling lethargic or bored. I also wear it when I am feeling really confident. I will tend to wear more dramatic clothing with clear, bold lines and usually one powerful accent. It is a color associated with assertiveness and when I am faced with not feeling very confident I will also wear red to shock me into it. I will avoid wearing red when I am feeling angry and will revert to blue to calm me down enough that I can sit and meet the anger in a responsible way. I actually use red to light my fire, literally!!!

**Magenta** - Magenta is a blending of red and violet and a dash of white or pink (and violet is a combination of red and blue). Magenta is a color of transition. (Note: although there are different color combinations that can bring about the color magenta, this is the one that I feel most clearly brings it about). It does not have a separate counterpart in the elements, however is a combination of the elements of fire, water, and metal with traits often referred to as the wizard, philosopher, and alchemist in Chinese medicine. It is a combination of the boldness of the dramatic with the softness of violet and a touch of white. My connection with Magenta coincided with my delving into spiritual studies that combined the influence of the elements of water, fire and metal (the philosopher, the wizard, and the alchemist). I had begun to soften my dress with adding more soft, clear flowing fabrics rather than straight form fitting clothing. It was the true beginning of the divine feminine emerging in me. I had begun yielding to the call of spirit and began embracing this call with how I was dressing. It was the beginning of my "letting go" of the masculine approach to living that I had been conditioned to while living in this culture. I feel that Magenta is a color that assists in our letting go of old limiting beliefs that hold us back from realizing our truth divine essence. It is interesting that in this 2013 spring season the stores seem to be focusing on the color Magenta (Fuchsia, Hot Pink) and that we have just passed through the end of the Mayan Calendar into the transformation of the Earth. Use Magenta to help you with this transition.

**Orange** – Orange quite honestly makes me happy. It lifts my spirits whenever I feel down and out. I wear it when I feel the need to be more sociable and playful and as an aid in negotiations I will use softer versions of orange such as terracotta and peach. Orange is the complement of blue on the color wheel and as such can help us snap out of a dream state into being more concrete when the need arises to begin to be more playful. It is the color associated with the Chakra located in the area of our sexual organs and as such it has been associated at times with creativity coming out of play. If you want to be more playful in the bedroom orange is a good color, however, it is best not to use it in a child's bedroom because it induces Play rather than sleep. Better to use blue in the bedroom to help with sleeping. Orange also gives the feeling that time is moving fast which is why many fast food restaurants use the color Orange – quick in and out and inexpensive. I have also found that orange can lift me up out of depression.

**Yellow-** As the color associated with the element of "Earth" yellow helps me to feel more compassion. In the Chakra system it is associated with the solar plexus and is a yang color. When I "can't stomach something" I recognize that I am not feeling very compassionate either towards myself or someone else. Wearing yellow often helps me with feeling more compassion and creating peace and harmony. As the color of the Sun it simply radiates peace and love. It is a nurturing color that I associate with sunshine. A bouquet of yellow flowers in your office can help to spur your creativity. However, too much yellow in a room can create tension. It is not easy on the eyes in large doses and I do not recommend wearing it if you are going to be making a presentation of more than 30 minutes. It could induce anxiety in the audience and because of this it is not a good color to use in prisons.

**Green** – Green is the color associated with the Heart Chakra, a color of balance and harmony. It is neither yin nor yang. It is neutral. As mentioned earlier it is the color associated with the Wood/Air element. It is also associated with security and safety. Balance and harmony foster security and as the color of money in the United States it is no accident that it is associated with security. Hospital scrubs often are green because it is also associated with healing. The heart is the center of the human body and is the medium between the lower physiological chakras and the upper spiritual chakras. It has a role to connect our bodies with our spirits-it is like a bridge. Green also gives the feeling that time is passing by slowly which is why a lot of fine dining restaurants decorate with forest green. However, it is not a good color for a prison because it makes time seem like it is passing by very slowly. Green, like the wood element, is associated with growth and doing as well and in this regard it is the "go" signal of our traffic lights. So, when feeling lethargic it is time to put on the green and get up and go!

**Blue** – On a beautiful clear day the sky is my favorite shade of deep royal blue. It has a calm aliveness about it that I cannot describe in words. There are many shades of blue as there are many shades of all the rainbow colors, and the calmness that blue brings with it for me is so serene. As the color associated with water I am reminded of the two extreme qualities of water – ice and flow. When I am in need of calming down I wear blue and imagine its flowing, caressing movements. Water also solidifies as ice, and sometimes when I am fearful and feeling rigid, I will defer to wearing red to help melt away the fear. Blues are the complements of red and orange on the color wheel and they can play very important roles in healing. The coolness of blue can help with inflammations of various sorts. Often when I have a headache I will wear blue, and even think or look at the color blue to help me with that. Blue is the color associated with the Throat Chakra that houses our communication center and is associated with truth. You've heard the expression "true Blue". The American Flag is Red, White, and Blue (Power, Purity, and Truth). Surveys of many people have shown that blue is the most common favorite color.

**Indigo** – A very dark color I associate with the dark blue midnight sky. The darkness of the midnight sky enhances the brilliance of the silvery moon – which represents the divine feminine. It is mysterious and is the color associated with the Third Eye Chakra.

This is the opening to see and connect with the unknown/spirit. Hindu people often wear a bindi on their foreheads in between their eyebrows to help them connect with their God, (their trinity of Brahma. Vishnu, Shiva). Indigo is essentially navy blue and I also associate it with the depths of the ocean and mystery. Indigo and the third eye open the doors to spirit and creativity.

# Chapter 13

# *Your Toolkit*

## Favorite Outfit Exercise

*Put on some soft instrumental music as you do this exercise.*

Take a moment to remember what your favorite outfit is. This is the outfit that makes you feel beautiful and special. What color is it? What style is it? What is the texture? What is the line? Is it a print or a solid? Is it a dress, skirt and top, pants and top, gown, or a suit. For this exercise, please exclude sweats and active wear. How does it make you feel? Do you receive compliments when you wear it? If you do not have a favorite outfit you can skip on to the next question. If you do have a favorite outfit complete the next question after you complete this description.

What would you LOVE to wear if you truly did not care what anyone else thought? I am talking about your boss, your spouse, or your friends. And I am not interested in a response of sweats and active wear. We all like to let it all hang out! What I am looking for is what would make you feel like a goddess/god when you are wearing it. Please describe it in detail: color, style, texture, lines, etc.

# God/Goddess Questionnaire

You and your best girl friend are going to a party and you notice that she has lipstick on her teeth. What do you do about it? How do you feel about it?

-You would tell her as soon as you noticed it because you would want to be told if you had lipstick on your teeth and you like to present a neat well put together appearance?(Wood-Athena)

-You would feel that you were interfering with her space and not say anything because you wouldn't want to offend her or you might tell her right away because you feel sorry for her? (Earth-Demeter)

-You wouldn't even notice it, so there wouldn't be any reason to say anything. In fact, you would be surprised to learn that someone would even care if they had lipstick on their teeth! (Metal-Zeus)

-You would ponder whether or not to tell her because you would be fearful that she might get offended or you might not even notice because you were simply going with the flow of the moment and the conversation. (Water-Poseidon)

-You would crack up laughing at your friend because she had lipstick on her teeth and then tell her because you would want to be a good friend and your relationship with her is very important to you. (Fire-Aphrodite, Venus)

What would make you feel more light and airy in clothing and colors?

What is your dominant passion:
to do? (Wood) Athena
to be? (Metal) Zeus
to nurture?(Earth) Demeter
to communicate? (Fire) Aphrodite/Venus
to know? (Water) Poseidon

## Journey to Mt. Olympus:

Imagine yourself receiving an invitation to a ball on Mt. Olympus (home of the gods) and you need to make plans on how to get there. You have no idea where it is, yet you know that you have the choice of the mode of transportation to get you there. Would you:

take the Concord? (Wood) (Athena)
passenger plane? (Wood) (Athena)
by boat? or (Water) (Poseidon)
by bicycle? or (Earth) (Earth)
by horse/chariot? (Fire) (Aphrodite/Venus)
by Pegasus/Unicorn? (Metal) (Zeus)
Other – you name it.

What would you wear as you're traveling to get there?

a low cut top with form fitting leggings (red) (Fire) (Aphrodite/ Venus)
comfortable slacks and jacket, (green) (Wood) (Athena)
you would want to know what everyone else was wearing, but something flowing and fluid (blue) (Water) (Poseidon)
something stylish but in conservative colors small print and comfortable, probably jeans (yellow) (Earth) (Demeter)
something white, clean and comfortable (Metal) (Zeus)

What would you love to wear to the Ball?

A low cut figure hugging gown in a bright color-red or fuchsia (Fire) (Aphrodite/Venus)
Free flowing elegant loose comfortable pantsuit in white or off white (Metal) (Zeus)

Small print or pastel solid conservative gown, possibly belted with yellow (Earth) (Demeter)

Blue/green boldly striped gown, structured-dramatic, one shoulder (Wood) (Athena)

Pale blue gown, full and flowing with a possibly puddle look or trumpet at the bottom (Water) (Poseidon)

# A Journey to choose your color for the day:

## Tip Toe Through the Tulips

Put on some soft, instrumental music -

Close your eyes and imagine yourself slowly walking through the forest noticing all the beautiful trees, bushes, insects, and wild flowers along the path. Suddenly you come upon an open space; a meadow and as you now frolic through the meadow you notice ahead a field of beautiful tulips appearing in the distance-you become enraptured by the grouping of the various colors-the Sun is shining brightly and the sky is clear blue with a few puffy clouds. Looking more closely at the tulips you notice they have been arranged in a circular form in the middle of the meadow. There is one circular row of red tulips surrounding the outer edge, then 2 circular rows of orange tulips, followed by 3 circular rows of yellow tulips, and 4 circular rows of green tulips, and 5 circular rows of turquoise blue tulips; then 6 circular rows of indigo/navy blue tulips, and finally 7 circular rows of violet/purple tulips. This circular tulip garden is spinning and dancing in a beautiful cosmic dance - red to the left, orange to the right, yellow to the left, green to the right, turquoise blue to the left, indigo/navy blue to the right and finally violet/purple to the left. While watching this floral cosmic dance you notice one color vibrating towards your center above all the rest and suddenly only that color remains visible to you as it expresses to you your color connection to spirit for that day: is it red, orange, yellow, green, turquoise, indigo, or violet? Pick up the tulip in the color that stayed with you and hold it, feel its essence and begin to see your outfit for the day come together as you visit your closet and dresser drawers in search of clothing in that color.

# OR

## An Elemental Journey to choose what color to wear:

Relax and play some instrumental slow music as you take this short journey to discover which color is in tune with your energy each day. Sit in a comfortable chair, close your eyes unless you need to read this until you can memorize it, take in a few deep breaths, clear your mind of thoughts, and relax into a short visualization: It would be nice if someone could read it to you in a soft voice as you relax:

Imagine yourself walking through a very thick green forest noticing all of the foliage along the way. Take in the sounds, smells and feel of the breeze and or sun. What do you see? Is the green grass making you desire to take off your shoes and frolic in it? Do you need a push to stop procrastinating that project you have been putting off? Or don't you notice it at all? Notice if there are any animals in the area. Is the bright blue sky with its' puffy white clouds grabbing your attention? As you are walking along you come to a small pond with beautiful clear ice blue water off to the side and then further in you notice that looking into it deeper it is black. Stay by the water for a while if you would like, do you feel like dipping your toes in it for a while or simply keep on walking. Have you been doing too much and need to relax and chill out a bit. Notice what appears to you as you are walking. Do you see the violet iris with its free flowing petals to your left? Do you feel the need to lighten up and stop thinking? How about the red roses clustered off to the left? Do you feel the need to connect and communicate with others? Are they stimulating your passion? What do they say to you? Suddenly you notice a patch of yellow daffodils – how do they make you feel today? Have you been beating yourself up over some mistakes and/or misunderstandings and need some compassion for yourself? Are you feeling blue today and need a pick me up? A little further ahead you notice a tree with a ring of orange tulips surrounding it. Do you need to work less and play more? What color feels in tune for you today? Red, Orange, Yellow, Green, Blue, Dark Blue/Black, or Violet or White.

# How do colors make you 'feel'?

This is an exercise in determining how each of the rainbow colors makes you feel in general. In this exercise we are not looking for your thoughts about the color, rather I am asking you to look inside for your feelings.

For example: Does it excite your passion or give you energy?
Does it make you happy?
Does it invoke sadness?
Does it make you feel confident?
Does it inhibit you?
Does it make you feel ill?
Etc., etc., etc.,

You may need a piece of clean white paper to assist you in this exercise along with a color wheel. Sit quietly with some peaceful non-lyrical music playing softly in the background. When you are ready, place the red color from the wheel on the paper while hiding the other colors with another piece of white paper and observe it looking inside to your inner being and ask spirit how it makes you FEEL. When you receive the answer write it down. Proceed with each of the next colors in rainbow order, which are: red, orange, yellow, green, blue, indigo(dark navy), violet and do the same thing. After completing each rainbow color consider how white, black, and browns make you feel as well, and write that down. Both positive and negative feelings are important. What you are doing here is getting in touch with your own feelings about the colors and you will learn how to use them to help balance your energy on any given day.

### Healing negative feelings about colors:

Next you can work with the colors that you have negative feelings about:

Is there a negative story connected to your feelings about a color? If so, make a note of it and then do the following exercise for each of those negative stories about a color(s) thoughts/feeling and go deeper into to them to bring them into the light after you have completed your likes and dislikes feelings:

Note: STOP AND do this exercise NOW before reading on so that you dot not create any expectation of the outcome. Sit quietly and with the color you dislike, put your full attention on your physical body below the neck and notice where there is any discomfort. Drop any story you have attached to the color. The story is what causes the pain and suffering. If the story pops up, simply notice it and drop it. Place your full attention on this physical discomfort and notice what the emotion is underneath the physical discomfort without the story. When you identify the emotion go deep into the emotion and look to see what is underneath that emotion, once you identify that deeper emotion go deeper to identify the emotion that is under the previous emotion until you cannot go any deeper and notice what you notice. (Do this until you notice peace, compassion, clarity, love, or simply no-thing) You will see that underneath all of your stories about the color either there is something wonderful like love, clarity, peace, and compassion or there is just nothing! And therefore, you now can look at, wear, and feel great about wearing that color and using its' wonderful energy to assist you when your spirit needs it.

# Color Reinforcement Reminders

I am repeating to help you remember to connect with each of the colors and to reinforce with you that there are no bad colors!..:

Each of the rainbow colors is affiliated with one of the 7 chakras in the body. Red - root chakra located at the base of spine or tailbone, Orange-Sacral chakra located in pelvis area, Yellow-solar plexus located in the stomach area, Green - Heart chakra located in the heart area, Blue-throat chakra located in the throat area, Indigo blue-third eye chakra located in the brow area above the base of the nose, and Violet or white - Crown chakra located at the crown of the head. It is very likely that the chakra associated with the color your journey disclosed is the one that may need balancing on that day, so why not listen to that calling and wear that color for the day. Everything I have learned about the Chakras and the colors that are associated with them points to the relative masculine and feminine energies each of them represents. The lower Chakras, which I will call "Yang" or masculine - root, sacral and solar plexus relate more to humanity's outer physical energies, are connected by the Heart Chakra, at center-neither yin nor yang, to the upper Chakras "Yin" or feminine - throat, third eye, and crown Chakras. As most of us know, the yin/yang symbol is a circle divided in half by a curved line with half black(yin) and half white (Yang) each with a dot of the opposite color in the widest point. This tells me that the dominant masculine energy also needs a bit of feminine energy and vice versa in order that we maintain balance with energy. Another interesting fact is that without both darkness and light we cannot see color. There is an experiment you can do with a prism and some black and white checked wheels on paper to prove this. Without the black and white checks the colors cannot be reflected through the prism. Each of the rainbow colors can also be categorized as yin or yang (feminine or masculine) and its opposite on the color wheel (or its complementary color) would be the added dot in the symbol. I have added the color "magenta" because it is a color that falls between red and violet and is considered a color of the highest order. And it seems to me it's no accident that its complement is Green - the color that represents the heart Chakra. For me, magenta also seems to connect the rainbow and chakras in a unified circle. According to Theo Gimbel in his "The Colour Therapy Workbook", magenta has a therapeutic use of facilitating changes, freedom, letting go of old habits no longer applicable and assists with the final transition into spirit at the correct time. The relative intensity of a color (how bright or soft a color is) also generates energy-bright are more outer, masculine while pastels are more inner/feminine.

| COLOR | COMPLEMENT |
|---|---|
| Magenta (N) | Green (N) |
| Red (M) | Bluegreen (F) |
| Orange (M) | Blue (F) |
| Yellow (M) | Violet (F) |
| Green (N) | Magenta (N) |
| Blue (F) | Orange (M) |
| Indigo (F) | Gold (M) |
| Violet (F) | Yellow (M) |
| White (M) | Black (F) |
| | |

M=Masculine
F=Feminine
N=Neutral

# Determining your causative factor-
# An Elemental Survey

With an open mind and an open heart review the following and circle to most dominant attribute that applies to you in each block. This may come to you in a flash or you may have to ponder a while but please do not overanalyze.

| *Way of Knowing: Circle one: Do you:* | *Your scent without perfume: Circle one:* |
|---|---|
| <ul><li>Gather lots of information (E)</li><li>Rely on intuition (F)</li><li>See both the broad perspective and focus on details (W)</li><li>By just being (M)</li><li>Trial and error (A)</li></ul> | <ul><li>Rotten, compost, dead animals (W)</li><li>Scorched (burned) (F)</li><li>Rancid, bad butter, urine (A)</li><li>Putrid, sulfurous, ammonia (M)</li><li>Fragrant (E)</li></ul> |
| *Emotional Extremes that best describe you: Circle one* | *Sound of your voice: Circle one:* |
| <ul><li>Profound sympathy – self absorbed (E)</li><li>Passion &joy – heartless & cold (F)</li><li>Clear & flowing-fear/ terror of being wrong (W)</li><li>Awe & wonderment – isolated & lonely (M)</li><li>Hopeful, organized & direct – angry, jealous and frustrated (A)</li></ul> | <ul><li>Laughter. Inability to laugh, or inappropriate laughter (F)</li><li>Groaning (W)</li><li>Shouting (A)</li><li>Weeping (M)</li><li>Singing (E)</li></ul> |

| <u>**Source of Security: Circle one**</u> | <u>**Dominant Season: Circle one:**</u> |
|---|---|
| • Determining & appreciating the worth of all things (E) <br> • Making & maintaining relationships (F) <br> • Having clear boundaries and knowing the answers (W) <br> • Being still & silent – making things simple (M) <br> • Completion of whatever needs to be done (A) | • Winter (W) <br> • Summer (F) <br> • Spring (A) <br> • No time – timeless (M) <br> • Autumn, late summer (E) |
| <u>**Passionate about: Circle one**</u> | **<u>Key</u>** |
| • To enrich & nourish – wanting it all (E) <br> • Wanting to communicate & feel close to others (F) <br> • Wanting to know (W) <br> • Wanting to just be (M) <br> • Just Do It – wanting to do (A/W) | W=Water <br> A/W=Wood/Air <br> F=Fire <br> E=Earth <br> M=Metal |

| **_Can be Obsessive about:_** _Circle one_ | **Nourishing Relationships** |
|---|---|
| • To have (E)<br>• To be close (F)<br>• To make things clear & precise (W)<br>• To make it simple (M)<br>• To achieve (A/W) | F nourishes E<br>A nourishes F<br>W nourishes A/W<br>M nourishes W<br>E nourishes M |
| **_Best Time of Day: Circle one_** | **Restraining Relationships** |
| • Late afternoon (E)<br>• Dusk, twilight (F)<br>• Dawn (W)<br>• None (M)<br>• Morning (A/W) | W restrains F<br>A restrains E<br>F restrains M<br>E restrains W<br>M restrains A/W |

Ideally, all of your answers will fall within the same letter. You might need to talk with friends to get help with the physical attributes of color around the eyes and mouth, smell, and sound of voice. The physical attributes are the main determining factors. However, when you add up the others you will see how they guide you to see how you operate in the world of form and where you go in and out of balance emotionally. Because our emotions change frequently it is often difficult to use the feelings as the determining factor. The physical attributes, if able to see and truly notice, are more accurate in my experience. Once you determine your causative factor, you can work with the therapeutic colors to use when your energy is out of balance, keeping in mind that you can also combine them with the healing properties and meanings and messages of the 7 Chakra colors as well. *(Note: the "A" when used alone also refers to the "AW" and is the Wood/Air element.)*

# *Conclusion*

## *Spirit, Body, Mind*

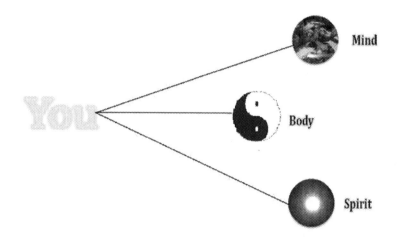

Which part of you that you have your attention on most of the time often will influence your total experience of life. Each part has a role in your healing and happiness. Fashion in the form of your clothing and color choices has a place of influence in all 3 areas. We need to integrate all 3 areas in order to have a fulfilling life and to experience true freedom. Fashion is one tool to help lead you to freedom. You now have a 'toolkit' to help you realize your divine essential true nature. You are FREE to work with it in any way that suits you. Don't worry about what you want the outcome to be. Your divine essence with come through as your masks fall away.

All of the above information has been provided by me based on my experiences in life and are the steps that have lead me to experience peace, love and freedom. None of the ideas are meant to put you in a box - I purposely did not give you an exact "'form'-ula" for you to determine who you are or how to dress, because it is up to you to discover that for yourself. Take and use what feels true for you and throw the rest away.

Find a teacher to help you go deeper than where this work takes you if you are so inclined. And remember- Clothes Encounters of the Divine Kind was written souly (pun intended) to help you shed the masks (veil of illusions) that our conditioning by society, the media and the fashion industry has created in an effort to control us at the expense of hiding our divinity.

Save this book and re-read it a year or two after working with the ideas and suggestions in it and see what masks have dropped away.

"Who Am I?" you might ask. "I AM". I AM Awake. I AM Pure Love. I AM Free. I AM Awareness. And I AM DIVINE. – in essence – I AM a divine being having a human experience. Who are you?

My wish for you is that you are able to transcend your own EGO to truly "see yourself" (i.e., Feel yourself) as the Love you are so that you too will be free.

Love and Namaste,
Diane Donato

# Bibliography

Books:

Beinfield, L.Ac., Harriet; Korngold, L.Ac, O.M.D.,Efrem. *Between Heaven and Earth, A Guide to Chinese Medicine. Random House of Canada Publishing.* Toronto, Canada

Birch, Cheryl S. *Rainbow Personality™ Developing Personal Style Consultant Handbook.* Modesto, California. 1988

Bolen, M.D., Jean Shinoda. *Goddesses in Everywoman.* New York, NY. Harper Perennial 2004

Bolen, M.D., Jean Shinoda. *Gods in Everyman,* New York, NY. HarperCollins Publishers, Inc., 1989

Gimbel, Theo. *The Colour Therapy Workbook,* Rockport, MA, USA, Element, Inc.1993

Gimbel, Theo. *Healing With Color And Light,* New York, Fireside 1994

Hauschka, Dr. *A guide to Dr. Hauschka Skin Care Preparations,* Wyoming, Rhode Island 1991

Ruiz, Don Miguel. *The Four Agreements,* San Rafael, California. Amber-Allen Publishing 1997

Williamson, Marianne. *A Return to Love,* New York, Harper Collins 1992

Oral Traditions and Various Teachings regarding Chinese and Tibetan medicine from: Howe, PhD., Keshav, Master Shaman and Teacher. Glastonbury, CT, USA 2003-2014